THE PENTATEUCH
MY FIRST HUNT
FOR THE HOLY SCRIPTURES

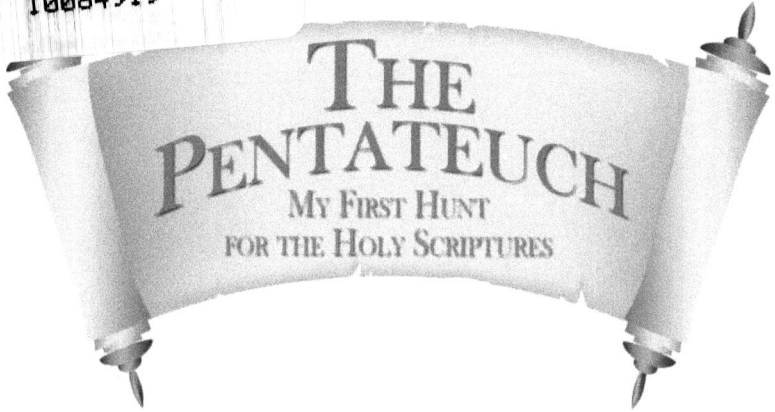

is presented to

_____

from

_____

on

_____

"Train up a child in the way he should grow: and when he is old, he will not depart from it":
Proverbs 22:6 (KJV)

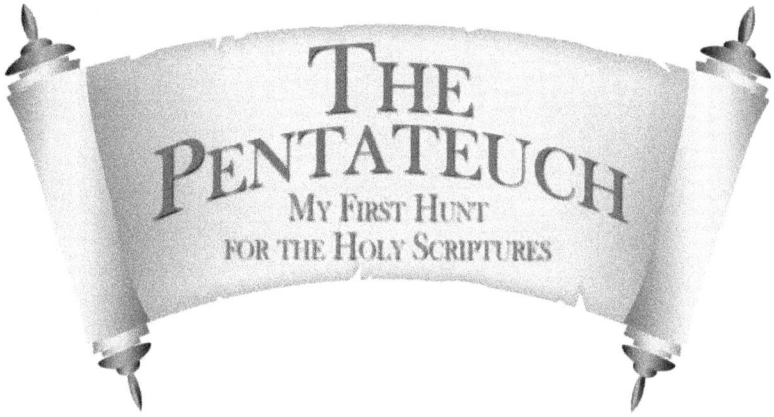

THE PENTATEUCH

MY FIRST HUNT FOR THE HOLY SCRIPTURES

AYANA S. HULL

Published By:
Jasher Press & Co.
www.jasherpress.com
customerservice@jasherpress.com
1.888.220.2068
New Bern, NC 28561

ISBN: 978-0692217788
ISBN-10:0692217789

First Edition
Printed and bound in the United States of America

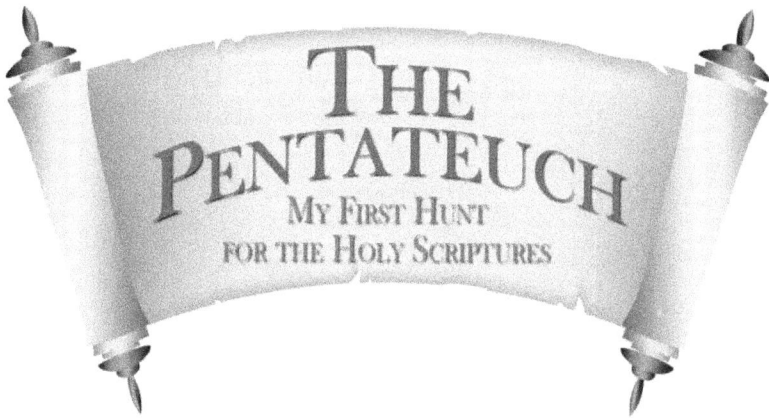

THE PENTATEUCH
MY FIRST HUNT
FOR THE HOLY SCRIPTURES

AYANA S. HULL

JASHER PRESS & CO.

FOREWORD
By Bishop John I. Cline

The Israelites were commanded to teach their children the word of God through every generation. They were commanded to ensure that future generations never forgot God and that they obeyed His commands and decrees. As Christians, we believe that through the shedding of Jesus' blood on the cross, we too are Israel and we must also carry forth this mandate through our generations as well.

In a world where it has become extremely challenging to reach young people through the word of God, and in a technological era where everything worldly is exciting, simple to understand and maneuver, the Church and its initiatives need to be innovative, exciting and youth-friendly in order to continue to attract and captivate young people into receiving the word of God.

Ayana has met this need for young people across the world. In The Pentateuch, she presents a practical and applicable approach to God's word. In all of our preaching and teaching, there still remains an uncaptured audience of youth without an understandable and easily digestible presentation of the Holy Scriptures. In these pages, the young will find easy to read, easy to understand representations of the word of God, which understanding and representation may otherwise be challenging for young people when using today's more popular translations of the Bible.

The stories of the Bible herein are brought to life and presented in an introductory, encouraging, exciting and refreshing way for young people to read and enjoy. In the lives and the situations faced by the biblical characters, the readers will see their mothers, fathers, sisters, brothers, aunts, uncles, nieces, nephews, cousins, friends and even themselves. Best of all, the word of God will minister to young people in a new and refreshing way. They will want to read their Bibles and will return again and again to the wisdom they gain from it. It is a work that will impact the rest of their lives.

The New Life Baptist Church is pleased to partner with Ayana on this project as we fulfill the Great Commission, teach the word of God, make young disciples, present unity and impact the lives of the young in a God desiring way.

ACKNOWLEDGEMENTS

My Heavenly Father—when You downloaded this idea in my spirit, it was a daunting task. I responded immediately in a Moses like way: "Me, I do not have the time. Where will I find the time?" Your response to me was, "If you make the effort, I will create the time for you!" You are certainly not a God that can lie! I hope that young people find The Pentateuch interesting and are able to read, understand, process and meditate on the word of God in a youth-friendly manner.

Peggy Clyne—thank you so much for your labour of love in sharing your time to edit The Pentateuch. May God continue to bless your hands, increase your wisdom and multiply your fruitful years.

Celia Georges—a heart-felt thank you for agreeing so willingly and enthusiastically to edit this work. I pray continuous blessings upon you eternally and may your rewards exceed your efforts.

My beautiful children, Rikkiya and Rikkoi—thank you for all your support, love, encouragement and understanding as I continue to walk in my God-ordained purpose. I thank God for you and I love you both dearly. Reach for the moon and always allow God to order your steps.

My humble parents, Nelson and Coreen Hull—thank you for being wonderful parents. Thank you for raising my brother and me in the fear and admonition of God. I was young but now that I am older, I can say with conviction that there is no better inheritance than a Godly inheritance. Daddy, thank you for never believing that I had done well enough in anything! Mommy, thank you for stepping in and protecting us when he kept insisting on pushing us past the limit!

My only brother and sibling, Kareem-Nelson—you are my number one fan. You are a brother that sticketh closer than a friend and I love you dearly. Thank you for all your support, love and assistance and for being a great male role model for my children. I pray that God enlarges your territory quickly!

My dear friend, John—you are truly a breath of fresh air. Thank you for all your encouragement, your support, your confidence in me and for sharing your precious time. You are truly a great inspiration to the lives you touch. I pray that your latter rain floods you with abundant happiness.

I love you all.

BEFORE THE BEGINNING &
THE BOOKS OF LAW

The Pentateuch contains fifty-four stories, the last fifty-three of which are taken from the first five books of the Bible, Genesis–Deuteronomy. Those books are also called the Pentateuch—meaning the first five books. The first story in The Pentateuch, which provides a brief introduction of God and Lucifer (before the beginning of human life on earth), constitutes the fifty-fourth story. The five books of the Pentateuch are referred to as the books of law as they record the instructions given to the Israelites through Moses which the Israelites were to follow. History records that these first five books were written by Moses, except for the last portion of Deuteronomy (which speaks about Moses' death). These first five books not only set out the creation story and lay down the laws for the Israelites, whilst recording their journey from Egypt to the Promised Land, but also lay the foundation for the coming of Jesus Christ in the New Testament, as they reveal the Israelites as the people chosen by God, the people that would benefit from the covenant He made with Abraham and the people through whose lineage the Messiah (the savior of sinners) would come.

Whilst it is a book that any person of any age can read and understand, it was particularly written with a pre-teen, teen, young-adult target audience in mind. It is an introduction only and is not intended to be a full treatment of the Pentateuch. In order to provide clarity and understanding to the target audience, the King James Version and the New International Version of the Holy Bible were relied upon and all quotations herein are credited to those versions of the Holy Bible as applicable. It is my hope that the young finds The Pentateuch to be a good biblically-based resource which can aid them in their daily lives and I pray that The Pentateuch fills the void it was intended to fill as well as assist in leading young lives, in particular, to Christ.

CONTENTS

BEFORE THE BEGINNING

God

God is a perfect, spiritual being who has never sinned or done anything wrong and is blameless. That is why He is the Holy of holies. He has always existed. Before there was anything, there was God. He is the ultimate Being of all beings. He is omnipotent—all powerful. He is omniscient—knows everything. He is the Most High God higher than all other gods. He exists not by birth or by creation. He is self-existent. He is eternal/everlasting and cannot be destroyed. This means that He existed through all time and will last through all time. He is alpha and omega. This means that He is without a beginning or an end. He is unchangeable, and as a result, He is unaffected by the passage of time and events. He is supernatural and cannot be explained or ascertained by natural law and logic. His majesty and power cannot be contained within this tiny paragraph of this chapter, as God is beautiful beyond any superlative descriptors fashioned by man and truly too marvelous for words!

Lucifer

Before the creation of man (woman and man in this context), God lived in Heaven with the angels He had created. Heaven is an eternal place which knew no concept of time (i.e. night, day nor season). He had many angels but Lucifer was classified as the highest ranking of all the angels and was created with tremendous powers and gifts. Lucifer was created by God as a cherub, the most powerful of God's angelic beings and walked amongst fiery stones. He was described in Ezekiel 28:12-14 as a model of perfection, full of wisdom, and perfect in beauty. He was adorned with precious stones—ruby, topaz, emerald, onyx, jasper, sapphire, turquoise and beryl. His tabrets and pipes were made of gold. In the Bible, the reference to tabrets and pipes is interpreted to mean instruments of worship.

Lucifer was the chief musician and worship leader in Heaven.

Lucifer's Pride
Lucifer's pride took control of him. He was not content in his position as the highest of the angels. He wanted to be God, and not just a servant of God. He said in his heart that he would ascend to Heaven and raise his throne above God's throne; that he would sit enthroned on the mount of assembly and would ascend above the tops of the clouds. He wanted to make himself like the Most High: Take a look at Isaiah 14:12–15 for a full treatment of Lucifer in this regard.

God found wickedness in him. Lucifer's heart became proud on account of his beauty and he corrupted his wisdom because of his splendor: Ezekiel 28:15–17. He became filled with violence and he sinned, so God drove him from the mount of God and expelled him from Heaven, together with one-third of the angels that were following him and supporting his sinful actions. Sin therefore began in the spiritual realm even before earth and human beings were created.

Name Change
After Lucifer was thrown out of Heaven, his name was changed to Satan. Lucifer is also known as the Devil. The angels that were thrown out with him are now called demons. Since then, Satan and his demons have been confined to the spirit world but have been wreaking havoc on earth from this spirit world. Satan continues in his rebellion or disobedience and he is diametrically opposed to God and His plans.

God's Future Plans
God then decided to create man, a class of human beings (not angels) who would love Him, serve Him and obey

Him. Created man was intended to live forever and not die, provided that he/she did not sin. Jesus was God's redemption plan for created man if created man did sin. As we will see, created man did indeed sin and God then had to implement the redemption plan by sending Jesus to die for created man's sin. Jesus then became God's representative in the earth after man sinned. Satan is therefore opposed to the teachings of Jesus and wants people to follow him and his evil ways instead of Jesus and Jesus' righteous ways.

The Differences between Jesus and Satan

Jesus is the son of God who took human form to die on the cross to save humanity from their sin (which Satan aided and abetted in the first place). Jesus' purpose is to lead people to salvation by freeing them from sin whilst Satan's purpose is to keep people enslaved to sin so that he can lead them to eternal punishment. Jesus sacrificed Himself because of love, whilst Satan on the other hand is motivated by vengeance. Because Jesus is love, He encourages His followers that they should be known by their love, joy, peace, patience, kindness, goodness, faithfulness, gentleness and self-control and these are the fruit that Christians should bear from their spirit-led life. However, those who follow Satan will have as their experience, amongst other negative influences, jealousy, envy, idolatry (worshipping other gods beside God), witchcraft, sexual immorality (e.g. adultery and fornication), hatred, discord, rage, selfish ambition, impurities and dissension. Followers of Jesus will be saved and live forever with God in Heaven upon His return, whilst those who follow Satan will be lost and will suffer with him in Hell forever.

STORIES OF GENESIS

Genesis is the title given to the first book of the Bible. It is appropriately named as the meaning of the word is 'beginning' or 'origin'. It is widely accepted that the book of Genesis together with the four books of the Bible following Genesis were written by Moses. These first five books are called the books of law or the Pentateuch. The book of Genesis records the beginning of the universe, the creation of man and woman, the creation of animals, it introduces the fallen angel, Lucifer, now called Satan (in the form of a serpent) and introduces the issue of temptation which in turn brings about the beginning of sin.
It displays efforts to redeem man and identifies the seed or blood line through which Jesus, the redeemer of man would come. It describes the beginnings of history, the life of Abraham, Isaac, Jacob and Esau and ends with the powerful story of Joseph. The stories of Genesis are intended to provide an introduction to powerful Bible stories from which important principles, core values and life lessons can be learnt.

CREATION

In the Beginning
In the beginning (**or when time began**), the earth was formless and empty. There was no light or living organism on earth.

Day 1 – Creation of Day and Night
So God decided to create the heavens and the earth. He said, "Let there be light" and light appeared. God was pleased with this and He called the light 'day' and the darkness which remained, He called 'night'. As a result, we had a morning and an evening which was referred to as the first day.

Day 2 – Creation of the Sky
After the first day, the waters on earth (both in the sky and on land) were gathered together in one place. On day two, God said, "Let there be an expanse between the waters to separate water from water." **An expanse is a wide area or surface**. Once the expanse was created, the Lord called the expanse 'sky'. He did no more work on day two.

Day 3 – Creation and Separation of Seas and Land
Once God created the sky, all that remained scattered beneath the expanse He had called sky, was water. So God said, "Let the water under the sky be gathered to one place and let dry ground appear." And exactly as God commanded it, it happened. He called the dry ground land and the gathered waters He called the seas. When God saw what He had done, He liked it and said it was good. He then commanded the land to produce seed-bearing plants of every kind and fruit-bearing trees of every kind. The dry land obeyed God's command and produced the seed-bearing plants and the fruit-bearing trees.

Day 4 – Creation of Lights in the Heavens
God created lights in the sky to separate day and night and to demarcate seasons. He said, "Let there be lights in the expanse of the sky to separate day from night and let them serve as signs to mark seasons and days and years and let them be lights in the expanse of the sky to give light on the earth." He made two great lights; one was greater than the other. The greater one was to govern the day (the sun) and the lesser one to govern the night (the moon). These two lights separated the day from the night. God also made the stars and He saw that it was good.

Day 5 – Creation of Sea Animals and Birds
Then God decided to create animals of the seas as well as birds. He said, "Let the water teem (i.e. to be full of, abound, swarm) with living creatures, and let birds fly above the earth across the expanse of the sky." All the creatures of the seas were created according to their own kind and every winged bird of its own kind was created also. When God saw that it was good, He blessed His creations and commanded them to be fruitful and increase in number and to fill the water in the seas. He also commanded the birds to increase on the earth.

Day 6 – Creation of Land Animals
God said, "Let the land produce living creatures according to their kind: (i) livestock (e.g. cattle, pigs, poultry); (ii) creatures that move along the ground (e.g. lizards, snakes, iguanas); and (iii) the wild animals (e.g. lions, tigers, bears, monkeys, wolves), each after its own kind." Livestock, the creatures that move along the ground and the wild animals were created according to their own kind and when He saw His creation, He liked it.

Man

Then God decided to make man. He said, "Let us create man in our own image, in our likeness, so that they may rule over the fish in the sea and the birds in the sky, over the livestock and all the wild animals and over the creatures that move along the ground." God therefore made man in His own image and He created man as male and female. He also created man as a creature superior to any other creature He had created.

Reproduction

God blessed man (male and female) and commanded them to be fruitful and increase in number; to fill the earth and to have dominion or authority over it. He commanded man to rule over the fish of the sea and the birds of the air and over every living creature that moved on the ground.

Food

Then God told man that he had every seed-bearing plant on the face of the whole earth and every tree that had fruit with seed in it. He commanded man to use the trees for food. To the beasts of the earth and all the birds of the air and all the creatures that move on the ground, He gave every green plant for food and **the ecosystem** operated exactly as God had said.

Day 7 – Day of Rest

After the heavens and the earth were completed in their great splendor, the Lord finished His work that He had been doing and He rested. God therefore blessed the seventh day and made it holy, because on this day He rested from all the work of creating that He had done.

ADAM AND EVE
(*First Man and Woman*)

Adam and Eve

Adam and Eve were the first two people God created. They lived in a place called the Garden of Eden. In order to create Adam, God formed him from the dust of the ground and breathed into his nostrils, the breath of life. Once God had breathed the breath of life into Adam's nostrils, Adam became a living being. Adam was then placed in the Garden of Eden by God. It was his home. Adam's job was to work the garden and take care of it. A river watering the garden flowed from Eden.

The Forbidden Tree

The Garden of Eden was beautiful. God placed all kinds of trees that were beautiful to the eye and which produced good tasting food in the Garden of Eden. However, in the midst of the garden, He also placed two trees which were known as (a) The Tree of Life and (b) The Tree of Knowledge of Good and Evil. God commanded Adam that he could eat freely from every tree in the Garden of Eden, but that he must not eat from the Tree of Knowledge of Good and Evil, for if he did, he would die.

Adam Names the Animals

God formed all the beasts of the field and all the birds of the air out of the ground and brought them to Adam to be named and whatsoever Adam named them, that was their name. So Adam named the livestock, the birds of the air and all the beasts of the field.

God Creates Eve

After God created Adam, He said that it was not good for Adam to be alone so He decided to make a helper that was suitable for Adam. In order to form the helper, God caused

Adam to fall into a deep sleep; and whilst Adam was sleeping, He took one of Adam's ribs and closed up with flesh, the place from which He took the rib. Then God made a female human being from the rib He had taken out of Adam and brought her to Adam. Adam said in response, "This is bone of my bones and flesh of my flesh; she shall be called woman, for she was taken out of man." Adam called his wife Eve because she would become the mother of all living things. It is for this reason and because of the creation of Adam and Eve in this manner that a man will leave his mother and father and be united with his wife and the two will become one flesh. **It is important to note that when God united Adam and Eve, the man and his wife were naked but they had no knowledge of it, so their nakedness did not make them ashamed. However, Eve had an encounter with Satan, who appeared in the guise of a serpent in the Garden of Eden which would cause severe consequential problems for her and Adam and, as we will see, the entire human race for that matter.**

THE FALL OF ADAM

Deception by the Serpent
The serpent was the craftiest of all the animals the Lord had made. He met Eve and asked, "Did God really say, 'You must not eat from any tree in the garden'?" Eve responded, "We may eat from every tree in the garden, but God did say, 'you must not eat fruit from the tree that is in the midst of the garden, and you must not touch it, or you will die.'" The serpent said to Eve, "You will not surely die, for God knows that once you eat of the fruit, your eyes will be opened and you will be like God, knowing good and evil."

The First Sin
Eve then listened to the serpent, disobeyed God's instruction and ate fruit from the forbidden tree as she saw it good for food and good for gaining wisdom. She ate some of the fruit and gave some to Adam to eat and he did eat. Both their eyes were opened and they then realised that they were naked, so they sewed fig leaves together in order to cover themselves.

Adam and Eve Hide from God
When Adam and Eve heard the sound of the Lord God as He was walking in the garden in the cool of the day, they hid themselves from Him amongst the trees. God called out to Adam asking where he was and Adam told God that he had hidden from Him because he was naked and afraid. God then asked Adam who had told him that he was naked and questioned him as to whether he had eaten of the tree from which he was commanded not to eat. Adam then blamed Eve for giving him the forbidden fruit. God turned to Eve for an explanation and Eve turned and blamed the serpent for deceiving her.

God's Curse upon the Serpent

For deceiving Eve, God cursed the serpent above all the livestock and wild animals. He told the serpent that it would crawl on its belly and eat dust all its life and that He would put enmity between the serpent and the woman and between the serpent's offspring and the woman's offspring. God said, "Her offspring will crush your head and you will bruise his heel." **This is the first indication in the Bible of the coming of Jesus and the resulting battle for souls between Jesus and the Satan.**

God's Curse upon Eve

God told Eve that He would greatly increase her pain whilst having children (so that she would give birth to children in pain). He also told her that her desire would be for her husband and that her husband would rule over her.

God's Curse upon Adam

God told Adam that because he had listened to his wife and had eaten from the tree in respect of which He commanded him not to eat, the following things would occur:

- Cursed would be the ground because of him and through painful toiling Adam would eat of the ground all the days of his life;
- The ground would produce thorns and thistles for Adam and he would have to eat the plants of the field;
- Adam would eat food by the sweat of his brow until he returned to the ground (died); and
- Since he was taken from the ground, he would return to the ground upon his death.

After God pronounced the curses, God made garments of skin for Adam and Eve and clothed them. God then said that man had become as God to know good and evil, so before man took also of the Tree of Life, ate it and lived forever, God sent Adam and Eve out of the garden to work the ground from which they were taken. He then placed, at the east of the Garden of Eden, cherubim (**the second highest order of angels, seraphim being the highest order of angels after Lucifer was cast out of Heaven**), and a flaming sword which turned every way, to keep the way (guard) of the Tree of Life.

CAIN AND ABEL
(*The First Children*)

Sometime after Adam and Eve left the Garden of Eden, Eve found herself conceived (pregnant) and eventually gave birth to Cain. She later conceived again and gave birth to another son, whom she named Abel. Cain was therefore the first son and child on earth and Cain and Abel became the first siblings.

Cain and Abel's Sacrifice
Cain was a tiller of the ground. He worked the soil and planted, raised and harvested crops (e.g. fruits and vegetables). His brother Abel was a shepherd and kept flocks. As time went by, they both brought an offering to the Lord. Cain brought some of the fruits of the soil as his offering to the Lord whilst Abel brought fat portions from some of the firstborn of his flock. The Lord was pleased with Abel's offering but was not pleased with Cain's offering. Cain became very angry and his face was very sad. The Lord asked Cain why he was angry; He scolded Cain and told him that if he did what was right, he would be accepted, but if he did not then sin would crouch/squat at his door. God warned Cain that sin desired to rule him but that he must master it.

The First Murder
Cain encouraged Abel to go out to the field. While they were both there, Cain attacked Abel and killed him. Then God asked Cain, "Where is your brother Abel?" Cain replied, "I do not know. Am I my brother's keeper?" God asked Cain, "What have you done?" "Listen!" God said, "Your brother's voice cries out to me from the ground."

God Curses Cain

God told Cain that he was under a curse and that he was driven from the ground, which had opened its mouth to receive Abel's blood from his hand. God warned Cain that going forward, when he worked the ground, it would no longer yield its crops for him. God also told him that he would be a restless wanderer on the earth. Cain complained to God, telling Him that his punishment was more than he could bear. Cain also complained to God that with that punishment anyone who found him would kill him. So God made it clear to him, that if anyone killed him, that person would suffer vengeance seven times over and God put a mark on Cain so that no one who found him would kill him. Cain therefore went out from the Lord's presence and lived in the land of Nod, which was east of Eden.

NOAH AND THE GREAT FLOOD

Giants in the Earth
When men began to increase in number on the earth and daughters were born to them, the sons of God (fallen angels) saw that the daughters of men were beautiful, and they married any of them they chose. Then the Lord said, "My Spirit will not contend with man forever, for he is mortal; his days will be a hundred and twenty years." Some biblical scholars believe that the Nephilim (giants) were on the earth in those days, as the union of the sons of God (fallen angels) and the daughters of men, produced giants. These children were said to be the heroes of old, men of renown.

Wickedness Found on Earth
Many, many years after creation, thousands of years even, God saw the wickedness of men on earth and He saw that every thought of man's heart was evil at all times. The earth had become corrupt in God's sight and was full of violence. God repented (He was sorry) that He had made man on the earth and God's heart was filled with pain. So He said that He would wipe mankind from the face of the earth, along with all living things. But Noah found favour in God's eyes. Noah was a descendant of Adam, through his son, Seth (whom Adam had procreated when he was 130 years old).

The Uprightness of Noah
Noah was righteous and upright and he was blameless amongst the people of his time. Noah walked with God. He had three sons, Shem, Ham and Japheth. The Lord told Noah that He was going to put an end to all people on earth because of their wickedness and that He would do it by flood. He instructed Noah to make an ark of cypress/gopher wood with specific measurements. He

31

instructed him to build rooms in it and coat it with pitch inside and out. The ark was to be 450 feet long, seventy-five feet wide and forty-five feet high. It was to have a roof and the ark was to be finished within eighteen inches of the top. Noah was to put a door in the side of the ark and build lower, middle and upper decks within it.

God explained to Noah that every living, breathing creature would perish by the flood. However, God established an agreement with Noah which allowed Noah, his wife, his sons and his sons' wives to go into the ark with him. Noah was also to bring into the ark two of all living creatures with him to keep them alive. He was further instructed to take seven of every kind of clean animal, a male and a female, and two of every kind of unclean animal, a male and its mate, and also seven of every kind of bird, male and female, to keep their various kinds alive throughout the earth. Noah was also instructed to take every kind of food that was to be eaten, and to store it away as food for him, his family and the animals. He did everything just as God commanded him.

The Flood
When the time came for the flood, God instructed Noah to get into the ark (with his entire family and all the animals and birds) and told him that in seven days, He would send rain on the earth for forty days and forty nights. Noah was six hundred years old at the time of the flood. God opened the floodgates of Heaven and rain fell on the earth for forty days and forty nights. The waters increased greatly on the earth and covered all the highest mountains, and the ark floated on the surface of the waters. Every living thing that moved on the earth perished—livestock, birds, wild animals, all the creatures that swarmed over the earth and all mankind. Although it rained for forty days and forty

nights (one month and just over a week), the waters continued to flood for 150 days (five months).

Then God remembered Noah and all the wild animals and the livestock that were with him and sent a wind over the earth so that the waters receded. At the end of the five months, the water level had significantly decreased and after about seven months, the ark eventually came to rest on the mountains of Ararat whilst the waters continued to recede. It was not until ten months had passed, that the tops of the mountains of Ararat became visible.

Forty days after the mountain tops became visible, Noah opened the window he had made in the ark and sent out a raven, and it kept flying back and forth until the water had dried up from the earth. Then Noah sent out a dove to see if the water had receded from the surface of the ground. However, the dove could not find any resting place to set its feet, which was evidence to Noah that there was water over all the surface of the earth, so it returned to Noah in the ark. After seven days, Noah sent out the dove again. This time, the dove returned with a freshly picked olive leaf in its beak, so Noah knew that the waters had receded from the earth. Noah, to be certain, waited yet another seven days and sent the dove out again but this time, the dove did not return to him. God then commanded Noah to leave the ark together with his wife, his sons, their wives and the animals, so that they could multiply on the earth and be fruitful and increase in number upon the earth.

Noah Builds an Altar to the Lord
After Noah left the ark, he built an altar to the Lord. He took some of the clean animals and clean birds and sacrificed burnt offerings on the altar. The Lord smelled the pleasing aroma and said in His heart: "Never again will I curse the ground because of man, even though every

inclination of his heart is evil from childhood, and never will I destroy all living creatures as I have done." The Lord said, "As long as earth endures, seedtime and harvest, cold and heat, summer and winter, day and night will never cease." God also established this agreement with Noah and his descendants.

First Rainbow

God then set His rainbow in the clouds and told Noah that it would be a sign of the covenant between God and the earth so that whenever He brought clouds over the earth and the rainbow appeared in the clouds, He would remember His covenant with Noah and all living creatures of every kind.

Noah Curses Canaan

Noah worked in the soil and planted a vineyard. One day he drank some wine from his vineyard and became drunk. He then went to lie down and was naked when he did so. Noah's son, Ham (who was the father of Canaan) saw his father naked and went to tell his brothers (Shem and Japheth), who were outside at the time. Shem and Japheth took a garment and laid it across their shoulders, then they walked with their backs turned toward their father and covered their father's nakedness. Of importance, when they covered Noah's nakedness, their faces were turned the other way so that they could not see his nakedness. Noah awoke from his wine and found out what his youngest son had done to him (seen his nakedness and sharing it with his brothers) and he cursed Canaan. He said Canaan would be the lowest of slaves to his brothers.

Noah Blesses Shem and Japheth

Noah blessed Shem and also declared that Canaan would be the slave of Shem. He then asked for God to extend the territory to Japheth and that Japheth might live in the tents of Shem and for Canaan to be his slave.

Noah's Death
Noah died when he was 950 years old. He lived 350 years after the flood.

THE TOWER OF BABEL

In the beginning and even after the days of Noah, the whole world had one language and a common speech. As men moved eastward, they found a place to settle in Shinar, Babylonia and settled there. They decided amongst themselves that they should make strong bricks and in the bricks they used tar for mortar. They decided to use the bricks to build themselves a city, with a tower that reached to the heavens, so that they could make a name for themselves and not be scattered over the face of the whole earth. But the Lord came down to see the city and the tower that the men were building and said, "If as one people they have begun to do this, then nothing they plan would be impossible for them." So the Lord confused their language so that they would not understand each other and scattered them from there all over the earth, and they stopped building the city. This is why it was called Babel—because there the Lord confused the language of the whole world and from there the Lord scattered them over the face of the whole earth.

ABRAM, SARAI AND LOT

Abram (whose name would later change to Abraham) was the son of Terah. Terah was a descendant of Shem (one of Noah's sons). Terah had two other sons together with Abram whose names were Nahor and Haran. Haran was Lot's father but Haran died leaving Lot to be taken care of by Terah (his grandfather). Terah took Abram, Abram's wife, Sarai (who was also Terah's daughter, Abram's half-sister and whose name would later change to Sarah) and Lot and proceeded to go to Canaan but settled instead, in a place called Haran. Terah, at the age of 205, died in Haran.

God's Call to Abram
God told Abram to leave Haran (his country and his people) and to go to a land which the Lord would show him. He told him that He would make him into a great nation, He would bless him and would make his name great. God told Abram that he would be a blessing and whoever cursed him, God would curse and that all people on earth would be blessed through him.

Abram left Haran at the age of seventy-five. He took his wife and his nephew, Lot with him and all the possessions and the people they had accumulated in Haran and set forth for Canaan. The Lord appeared to Abram and showed him the land that He planned to give to Abram's offspring, so Abram built an altar there (the site of the great tree of Moreh at Shechem) where the Lord appeared to him. Abram then continued toward the hills east of Bethel and pitched his tent (with Bethel on the west and Ai on the east). He also built an altar there and called upon the Lord.

Abram in Egypt
Whilst en route to Canaan, Abram went down to Egypt to live as there was a severe famine in the land. Now Sarai,

37

Abram's wife was a beautiful woman, so as he was about to enter Egypt, he told Sarai that she should say that she was his sister to the Egyptians so that he would be treated well for her sake, as Abram feared that the Egyptians would kill him so that they could take Sarai.

As Abram had perceived, when Pharaoh's officials saw Sarai's beauty, they praised her to Pharaoh (a Pharaoh was the name given to a king of Egypt in ancient times) and Sarai was taken into Pharaoh's palace. Pharaoh treated Abram well for Sarai's sake; for Sarai told them that he was her brother. Abram acquired sheep and cattle, male and female donkeys, menservants, maidservants and camels in Egypt. But the Lord inflicted serious diseases on Pharaoh and his household because of Abram's wife, Sarai. Pharaoh therefore, upon finding out the truth, summoned Abram and asked him why he had not told him that Sarai was his wife and why he had told them that she was his sister. Then Pharaoh told Abram to take his wife and he gave specific orders regarding Abram to his men. They sent him on his way with his wife and everything he had acquired whilst in Egypt.

The Separation of Abram and Lot
Throughout the journey from Haran to Egypt, Abram had become very wealthy in livestock and in silver and gold. Lot too, was moving about with Abram and had flocks and herds and tents. The land could not support both of them whilst they stayed together as their possessions were too great and arguments often arose between Abram's herdsmen and Lot's herdsmen. So Abram said to Lot, "Let's not have quarreling between you and me, or between your herdsmen and mine, for we are brothers. Is not the whole land before you? Let's part company. If you go to the left, I'll go to the right; if you go to the right, I'll go to the left." Lot saw that the Jordan was well watered and

38

beautiful so he chose for himself the whole plain of the Jordan, near Sodom and both men parted company. Abram lived in the land of Canaan.

After Lot left, the Lord told Abram that He would give him all the land surrounding him that he saw to the north and south and east and west. The Lord told Abram that He would make his offspring like the dust of the earth, so that if anyone could count the dust, then his offspring could be counted. God then commanded him to go and walk the length and breadth of the land that He was going to give to him. Abram therefore moved his tents and went to live near the great trees of Mamre at Hebron, where he built an altar to the Lord.

Abram Rescues Lot
War had broken out against Sodom and Gomorrah. The four kings that won the war seized all the goods of Sodom and Gomorrah and all their food. They also carried off Abram's nephew, Lot (who was living in Sodom) and all his possessions. When Abram heard the news, he gathered his most trained men and went to war against the four kings who had taken Lot. Abram won the war, recovered all the goods and brought Lot back together with all his possessions, the women and the other people. When Abram returned, the king of Sodom came out to meet him and the king blessed Abram and Abram's God for delivering the enemies into his hand.

Abram gave the king of Sodom a tenth of everything he had recovered, but the king refused, saying to Abram, "Give me the people and keep the goods for yourself." However, Abram refused to take anything from the king of Sodom. Abram said, "I have raised my hand to the Lord, God Most High, Creator of Heaven and earth, and have taken an oath that I will accept nothing from you, not even a thread or thong of a sandal, so that you will never be able to say, 'I made Abram rich.' I will accept nothing but what my men have eaten and the share that belongs to the men who went with me."

God's Covenant with Abram for an Heir

After the rescue of Lot, the Lord appeared to Abram in a vision saying, "Do not be afraid, Abram. I am your shield, and your very great reward." Abram then questioned God as to whether he would have any children to inherit his estate or whether Eliezer of Damascus would inherit his estate. The Lord assured Abram that Eliezer would not be his heir but a son coming from his own body would be his heir. The Lord took Abram outside to look up at the heavens to count the stars—if he could indeed count them, as, as many as the stars, so would his offspring be. Importantly, Abram believed the Lord and God credited it to him for righteousness. It is estimated that Abram was approximately eighty-six years old at the time of this initial promise.

God Reassures Abram

Abram questioned God as to how he would be sure that he could actually gain possession of Canaan, the land God had promised. So the Lord asked Abram to bring to him a heifer, a goat and a ram, each of which should be three years old, along with a dove and a young pigeon. Abram did as God asked. Abram fell into a deep sleep as the sun was setting and a thick and frightening darkness came over him. Then the Lord said to Abram, "Know for certain that your descendants will be strangers in a country not their own, and they will be enslaved and mistreated four hundred years, and afterward they will come out with great possessions. You however, will go to your fathers in peace and be buried at a good old age. In the fourth generation, your descendants will come back here, for the sin of the

Amorites has not yet reached its full measure." On that day the Lord made a covenant with Abram and said, "To your descendants I give this land, from the river of Egypt to the great river, the Euphrates."

HAGAR AND ISHMAEL

Sarai and Abram had no children. **Now it was the custom in those days (and still is today in certain parts of the world such as Africa and the Middle East) that men were allowed to marry more than one woman and the wives of wealthy men had maidservants.** Sarai was concerned that she had not borne her husband a child, so she agreed that Abram should have a child with her maidservant, Hagar, the Egyptian, so that she (Sarai) could build a family through her maidservant. **In modern day language, Hagar was used as a surrogate in a sense (a substitute for someone or something/replacing someone or something) for Sarai.**

Abram agreed and Hagar conceived. However, once Hagar knew she was pregnant she began to despise Sarai, her mistress and Sarai blamed Abram for her suffering and for the way she was being treated by her maidservant. Abram reminded Sarai that Hagar was her maidservant and that she could do with her whatever she thought best. Sarai then began to mistreat Hagar and Hagar fled from her. The angel of the Lord found Hagar near a spring in the desert, called her by name—Hagar, servant of Sarai, and asked her where she was coming from and where she was going. Hagar told the angel that she was running away from her mistress, but the angel of the Lord told her to go back to her mistress and to submit to her. He also told her that her descendants would be increased, so much so, that they would be too numerous for her to count. He also told her that the child she was carrying was to be called Ishmael, as the Lord had heard her misery. She was also told by the angel that Ishmael would be a wild donkey of a man, his hand would be against everyone and everyone's hand against him, and he would live in hostility toward all his brothers.

Hagar gave this name to the Lord who spoke to her and she said, "You are the God who sees me"—for Hagar said that, "I have now seen the One who sees me." That is why the well was called Beer Lahai Roi. It is still there, between Kadesh and Bered. So Hagar bore Abram a son, and Abram gave the name Ishmael to the son she had borne. Abram was eighty-six years old when Ishmael was born.

THE PROMISE OF ISAAC

Thirteen or so years after the birth of Ishmael (Abraham's son with Hagar), when Abram was ninety-nine years old, the Lord appeared to him and said, "I am the Lord God Almighty, walk before me and be blameless. I will confirm my covenant between me and you and will greatly increase your numbers."

Abram fell face down and God told him further that he would be the father of many nations and that his name would no longer be Abram but would be Abraham. Hence, the meaning of Abraham is father of many nations. God told him that He would make him very fruitful, He would make nations of him and that kings would come from him. God also told Abraham that He would establish His covenant with him and his descendants after him for the generations to come and that He would give Canaan to him and his descendants after him for an everlasting possession.

God further told Abraham that he was no longer to call his wife Sarai and that her name would be Sarah, that He would bless her and would give Abraham a son by her. She would be the mother of nations; kings of peoples would come from her. When Abraham heard it, he fell face down and laughed and said to himself, "Will a son be born to a man a hundred years old? Will Sarah bear a child at the age of ninety?" So Abraham said to God, "If only Ishmael might live under God's blessing."

God then re-confirmed to Abraham that Sarah would bear him a son and that his name was to be Isaac and that He would establish His covenant with Abraham and his descendants after him. As to Ishmael, God heard Abraham and said that He would make Ishmael fruitful and would greatly increase his numbers, he would be the father of twelve rulers and that He would make him into a great nation. However, His covenant would be with Isaac, whom Sarah would bear to him within a year (of when God had spoken).

Later on, the Lord appeared to Abraham in the heat of the day, whilst he was sitting near the great trees of Mamre at the entrance to his tent. Abraham looked up and saw three men standing nearby. He offered them water to wash their feet and encouraged them to rest under the tree. He then offered them something to eat. Whilst the men were eating, they asked him for his wife, Sarah. Sarah was in the tent as she had been preparing the food for the men to eat. Then the Lord said, "I will surely return to you about this time next year, and Sarah your wife will have a son."

Sarah was listening at the entrance of the tent, which was behind Abraham. She laughed to herself as she thought, "After I am worn out and my master is old, will I now have this pleasure?" The Lord asked Sarah why she laughed and He repeated what she had said. The Lord then asked, "Is anything too hard for God?" I will return to you at the appointed time next year and Sarah will have a son." Sarah was afraid so she denied that she laughed but the Lord knew that she did laugh and He confronted her and declared, "Yes, you did laugh."

SODOM AND GOMORRAH

Sodom and Gomorrah were two cities near the plain of Jordan. The people who lived there were wicked and sinned greatly against God. The Lord told Abraham that the outcry against Sodom and Gomorrah was great, that their sin was grievous and that His intention was to destroy them. Abraham questioned God as to why He would sweep up the righteous with the wicked. After some discussion between the two, God agreed with Abraham that if He found fifty righteous people in Sodom, He would not destroy it for the sake of the righteous. Abraham then reduced the number to forty-five and asked the Lord whether He would spare the whole place for the sake of forty-five. The Lord agreed that He would spare it for the sake of the forty-five that were righteous. Abraham further reduced the number to forty and the Lord agreed, and then thirty and eventually down to ten. And the Lord agreed that if He found ten righteous people in Sodom and Gomorrah, He would not destroy it for the sake of the ten. When the Lord finished speaking with Abraham, He left and Abraham returned home.

There could not be found ten people in all of Sodom and Gomorrah who were righteous, so the Lord sent angels to destroy the cities. The two angels that were sent by God to destroy Sodom and Gomorrah arrived in the evening. They met Lot at the gate of the city and Lot invited them into his home to wash their feet and to have dinner. At first they resisted but eventually, at Lot's persistence, they agreed to spend time at Lot's house. Whilst they were at Lot's house, all the men from every part of the city of Sodom, both young and old, surrounded Lot's house asking for the men who came to Lot's house that night. They asked Lot to send the men out so that they could have sexual relations with them. Lot went outside to meet them and shut the door behind him. He pleaded with them, "No, my friends. Don't do this wicked thing. Look I have two daughters who have never slept with a man. Let me bring them out to you, and you can do what you like with them. But don't do anything to these men, for they have come under the protection of my roof."

The men did not listen to Lot and told him to get out of the way. They said, "This fellow came here as an alien and now he wants to play judge! We'll treat you worse than them." So they kept bringing pressure on Lot and moved forward to break down the door. However, the men inside the door reached out and pulled Lot back into the house and shut the door. Then they struck the men who were at the door of the house, young and old, with blindness so that they could not find the door. The men told Lot to get out of Sodom, and to take his entire family (daughters and intended sons-in-law), as they were going to destroy the place. So Lot went out and spoke to his family (daughters and intended sons-in-law) and he told them to get out of Sodom as the Lord was about to destroy it, but his intended sons-in-law thought he was joking.

When dawn was about to break, the angels urged Lot to take his wife and his two daughters or he would be swept away when the city was punished. Lot still hesitated, so the angels grasped his hands, the hands of his wife and his two daughters and led them safely out of the city (as the Lord was merciful to them). Once they were out of the city, the angels said, "Flee for your lives! Don't look back, and don't stop anywhere in the plain! Flee to the mountains or you will be swept away!"

But Lot pleaded with them that the mountains were too far to travel to, as he would die on his way to the mountains. There was a town nearer to them that Lot asked permission

47

to run to, instead of the mountains. The angels agreed and granted his request. The angels told him to flee quickly to the town as they could not do anything in Sodom until Lot had reached the town. The town was called Zoar. By the time Lot reached Zoar, the sun had risen over the land.

Then the Lord rained down burning sulphur on Sodom and Gomorrah from out of the heavens. He overthrew those cities and the entire plain, including all those living in the cities and also the vegetation in the land. Lot's wife disobeyed the angels' instructions and she looked back. For her disobedience, she was turned into a pillar of salt. The next morning, Abraham saw Sodom and Gomorrah burning, with smoke rising from it like smoke from a furnace. But when God destroyed those cities of the plain, He remembered Abraham and He brought Lot out of the catastrophe that overthrew the cities where Lot had lived.

ABRAHAM PRETENDS THAT SARAH
IS HIS SISTER AGAIN!

Abraham continued to move along his journey and spent some time in a place called Gerar. Whilst there, he had an encounter with Abimelech, the king of Gerar. He told the king of Gerar that Sarah was his sister, so the king sent for Sarah and she was brought to him. But the Lord came to the king in a dream one night and told him that he was as good as dead because of the woman he had taken, as she was a married woman.

Abimelech pleaded with God that he was innocent as he did not know that she was a man's wife. God acknowledged his innocence and the clearness of his conscience and so kept Abimelech from sinning against Him. He commanded Abimelech to return Abraham's wife. He told him that Abraham was a prophet, that he would pray for him and he would live; but that if he did not return Sarah, he and all his family would die.

Early the next morning, Abimelech summoned all his officials and told them what had happened and they were very afraid. Abimelech then called Abraham and asked, "What have you done to us? How have I wronged you that you have brought such great guilt upon me and my kingdom? You have done things to me that should not be done. What is your reason for doing this?"

Abraham told him that he knew that the people in Gerar did not fear God and that he thought they would kill him because of his wife. Abraham told king Abimelech, "Besides, she is my sister, she is the daughter of my father but not my mother and she became my wife." He told the king that he asked Sarah to tell others everywhere they went, as God had him wander from his father's house, that she was his sister and that that was the way she was to show her love to him.

Abimelech brought sheep and cattle and male and female slaves and gave them to Abraham, and he returned Sarah, his wife to him. Abimelech also told Abraham that he could live anywhere in Gerar that he pleased. The king said to Sarah, "I am giving your brother a thousand shekels of silver. This is to cover the offense against you before all who are with you and you are completely vindicated." Then Abraham prayed to God and God healed Abimelech, his wife and his slave girls so that they could have children again, as God had closed up every womb in Abimelech's household because of Abraham's wife, Sarah.

THE BIRTH OF ISAAC

As God had promised, He was gracious to Sarah. Sarah became pregnant and bore a son to Abraham in his old age and at the very time God had promised him. Abraham was one hundred years old at the time of Isaac's birth. Abraham named the child Isaac (as God had commanded), and circumcised him when he was eight days old (as God had commanded Abraham as part of the covenant, that each male in his generation and males of anyone in his household or bought with his money must be circumcised at eight days old).

Speaking about the birth of her long awaited son, Sarah said, "God has brought me laughter, and everyone who hears about this will laugh with me." And she added, "Who would have said to Abraham that Sarah would nurse children? Yet I have borne him a son in his old age." Isaac grew and on the day that Isaac was weaned, Abraham held a great feast. Sarah saw Ishmael mocking and said to Abraham, "Get rid of that slave woman and her son, for the slave woman's son will never share in the inheritance with my son Isaac."

The matter distressed Abraham greatly because Ishmael was, after all, his son. But the Lord told Abraham to do as Sarah told him to do because it was through Isaac that Abraham's offspring would be reckoned. God assured Abraham that He would make Ishmael into a nation also, just because he was his offspring. Early the next morning, Abraham took some food and water and gave them to Hagar. He set them on her shoulders and sent her off with Ishmael (**biblical scholars have varying views on the actual age of Ishmael at the time**). She went on her way and wandered in the desert of Beersheba.

When the water was finished, Hagar put Ishmael under one of the bushes. Then she went off and sat down nearby, about a bowshot away, for she thought that she could not watch Ishmael die, so she began to sob. God heard Ishmael crying and the angel of God called to Hagar from Heaven and said to her, "What is the matter, Hagar? Do not be afraid; God has heard the boy crying as he lies there." The angel told Hagar to lift up Ishmael and take him by his hand for the Lord will make him into a great nation. Then God opened Hagar's eyes and she saw a well of water, so she went and filled her container with water and gave Ishmael to drink. God was with Ishmael as he grew up and he lived in the desert and became an archer. Whilst he was living in the Desert of Paran, his mother found him a wife from Egypt.

GOD TESTS ABRAHAM'S FAITH

Sometime after Isaac was born, God tested Abraham's faith. God told him to take Isaac, his only son (**by him and Sarah**) whom he loved, and go to the region of Moriah. God told him that when he reached the region, he was to sacrifice Isaac on one of the mountains that God would instruct.

Early the next morning, Abraham awoke and saddled his donkey. He took with him two of his servants and his son, Isaac. When he had cut enough wood for the burnt offering, he set out for the place God had told him about. On the third day, Abraham looked up and saw the place in the distance. He said to his servants, "Stay here with the donkey while I and the boy go over there. We will worship and then we will come back to you."

Abraham took the wood for the burnt offering and placed it on Isaac's shoulders whilst he, Abraham, carried the fire and the knife. As both of them went on together, Isaac asked, "Father, the fire and wood are here, but where is the lamb for the burnt offering?" Abraham answered, "God himself will provide the lamb for the burnt offering." And both continued on the journey.

When they reached the place God had told him about, Abraham built the altar and arranged the wood on it. He then bound his son, Isaac and laid him on the altar, on top of the wood. He then reached out his hand and took the knife to slay his son, but at the very moment, the angel of the Lord called out to Abraham from Heaven, "Abraham! Abraham!" When Abraham answered, the angel said, "Do not do anything to him. Now I know that you fear God because you have not withheld from me your only son." Abraham looked up and saw a ram in a thicket and he caught it by its horns. He went over and took the ram and sacrificed it as a burnt offering instead of his son. So Abraham called that place 'The Lord Will Provide'. And to this day it is said, "On the mountain of the Lord, it will be provided."

The angel of the Lord called to Abraham from Heaven a second time and said, "I swear by myself declares the Lord, that because you have done this and have not withheld your only son, I will bless you and make your descendants as numerous as the stars in the sky and as the sand on the seashore. Your descendants will take possession of the cities of their enemies, and through your offspring all nations on earth will be blessed because you obeyed me." Abraham then returned to his servants and they set off together, down from the mountains.

ISAAC AND REBEKAH
(Young Love)

Sarah lived to be 127 years old and then she died. She was buried in the cave in a field of Machpelah near Mamre (which is at Hebron) in the land of Canaan (which Abraham purchased from the Hittites as a burial site). Abraham was now old and well advanced in his years and the Lord had blessed him in every way. One day he asked the chief servant in his household to swear by the Lord, the God of Heaven and the God of earth, that he would not get a wife for Isaac from the daughters of the Canaanites but that he would go back to Abraham's country, Ur and get Isaac a wife from amongst Abraham's own relatives. **It is instructive to note that in those days, as is still the case in some places in the world, such as the Middle East, spouses were chosen for children by their parents or guardians**.

Abraham told the servant that the Lord would send an angel before the servant so that he could get a wife for Isaac from Abraham's own country. He told the servant that he was not to take Isaac back to his home country as the Lord had already promised to give Abraham and his descendants the land of Canaan. However, Abraham told the servant that if he should find a wife for Isaac and the woman did not want to come back with him, he would be released from the oath. The servant swore according to all that Abraham had requested.

The servant then took ten of Abraham's camels and left, taking with him all kinds of good things from Abraham's possessions. When he arrived at Ur, he prayed, "O Lord, God of my master Abraham, give me success today, and show kindness to my master Abraham. See, I am standing beside this spring, and the daughters of the townspeople are coming out to draw water. May it be that when I say to a girl, 'Please let down your jar that I may have a drink,' and she says, 'Drink and I'll water your camels too'—let her be the one you have chosen for your servant, Isaac. By this I will know that you have shown kindness to my master."

Before he had finished praying, Rebekah came out with her jar on her shoulder. Rebekah was a very beautiful sight to behold. The servant hurried to meet her and said, "Please give me a little water from your jar." "Drink my lord", she said, and quickly lowered the jar in her hands and gave him a drink. After she had given him a drink, she said, "I'll draw water for your camels too, until they have finished drinking." So she quickly emptied her jar into the trough, ran back to the well to draw more water, and drew enough for all the camels. Without saying a word, the man watched her closely to learn whether or not the Lord had made his journey successful.

When the camels had finished drinking, the servant took out gold and presented Rebekah with it and asked her whose daughter she was. Rebekah told him who her parents were. Then he asked whether there was enough room in her father's house for him to spend the night. When Rebekah assured him that there was, he bowed down and worshipped the Lord saying, "Praise be to the Lord, the God of my master Abraham, who has not abandoned his kindness and faithfulness to my master. As for me, the Lord has led me on the journey to the house of my master's relatives."

Rebekah ran to tell her parents what had happened and Abraham's servant was invited to the house by Rebekah's brother, Laban. After they had heard the servant's recap of the events that took place, Laban and Bethual (Rebekah's father) said, "This is from the Lord; we can say nothing to you one way or the other. Here is Rebekah; take her and go, and let her become the wife of your master's son, as the Lord has directed." The servant bowed to the ground again before the Lord. Then the servant brought out gold and silver jewelry and articles of clothing and gave them to Rebekah. He also gave expensive gifts to her brother and to her mother. Rebekah's family wanted her to remain with them ten days before she left for her new life but the servant asked them not to detain him any further as he wished to get back to his master. When Rebekah's view was sought, she agreed to go with the servant right away. The next morning, Rebekah, her maids and Abraham's servant set out to go back to Abraham and Isaac.

Meanwhile, back in the land of the Philistines, a part of Canaan, Isaac went out to the field one evening to meditate. As he looked up, he saw camels approaching. Rebekah also looked up and saw Isaac. She climbed down from her camel and asked the servant, "Who is that man in the field coming to meet us?" "He is my master," the servant answered. So she took her veil and covered herself. Then the servant told Isaac all that he had done. Isaac brought her into the tent of his mother, Sarah, and he married Rebekah. So she became his wife and he loved her; and Isaac was comforted after his mother's death. He was forty years old at the time.

Abraham also married again after Sarah's death and his second wife's name was Keturah. He had other sons whom he gave gifts while he was living, but left everything he owned to Isaac after his death. He also sent his other sons to live in a land in the east and away from Isaac. Altogether Abraham lived 175 years and then he died. He was buried with his wife, Sarah in the cave of Machpelah near Mamre at Hebron.

THE BIRTH OF JACOB AND ESAU
(*First Twins*)

Isaac and Rebekah had been married for nineteen years and they had no children. Isaac prayed to the Lord on behalf of Rebekah for she was barren and could not have any children. The Lord answered his prayer and Rebekah became pregnant. The babies jostled against each other within her and she said, "Why is this happening to me?" So she went to inquire of the Lord. The Lord said to her, "Two nations are in your womb, and two peoples from within you will be separated; one people will be stronger than the other, and the older will serve the younger."

When the time came for Rebekah to give birth, there were twin boys in her womb. The first to come out was red, and his whole body was like a hairy garment; so they named him Esau. After he came out, his brother came out, with his hand grasping Esau's heel; so he was named Jacob. Isaac was sixty years old when Rebekah gave birth to them. The boys grew up, and Esau became a skillful hunter, a man of the open country, while Jacob was a quiet man staying amongst the tents. Isaac, who had a taste for wild game, loved Esau, but Rebekah loved Jacob.

Once when Jacob was cooking some stew, Esau came home famished and pleaded with Jacob to give him some stew but Jacob replied that in order for Esau to eat the stew, Esau must sell him his birthright. Esau joked and said, "Look I am about to die. What good is the birthright to me?" But Jacob insisted that he swore to sell it to him. So Esau, **not appreciating or being concerned with the sacred meaning attaching to his birthright**, swore an oath to Jacob, selling his birthright to Jacob for a bowl of bean stew. Then Jacob gave Esau some bread and some lentil stew. He ate and drank, and then left. So Esau appears to have despised his birthright **as he sold his inheritance for a bowl of stew.**

What is a birthright? A birthright is referred to as a person's inheritance and was the right of the firstborn child in biblical times and is still so in many cultures and traditions. Historically, the firstborn would be given a double portion of his father's inheritance. If a man had three children, for the purposes of calculating the birthright, one child would be added and then the total number would be divided into four with the eldest child receiving two-fourths of the estate (which is half), and with the two remaining children receiving one-fourth each.

ISAAC ENCOUNTERS KING ABIMELECH

A famine arose in the land and Isaac went up to king Abimelech of the Philistines in Gerar. But the Lord appeared to him and told him not to go down to Egypt, that he should live in the land where God told him to live for a while and that God would be with him and would bless him. He confirmed to Isaac that He would give to him and his descendants all the land in the area of Canaan and that He would confirm the oath that He swore to his father, Abraham.

He told Isaac that He would make his descendants as numerous as the stars in the sky and that through his offspring all nations on earth would be blessed because Abraham obeyed Him and kept His requirements, His commands, His decrees and His laws. So Isaac stayed in Gerar. When the men at Gerar asked Isaac about Rebekah, like his father before him, he said that she was his sister. As she was so beautiful, he feared that if he told the truth, they would kill him on account of Rebekah. However, one day, after Isaac had been there a while, the king looked down from his window and realised based on their affection to each other, that Rebekah was Isaac's wife and not his sister. He summoned Isaac and questioned him as to why he had lied to them. Isaac explained that he had feared for his life. So Abimelech gave orders that anyone who molested Isaac or his wife would be put to death.

Whilst Isaac was in Gerar, the Lord blessed him and every seed he planted reaped a great harvest. He became rich and his wealth continued to grow until he became very wealthy. He had so many flocks and herds and servants that he began to become the envy of the Philistines. King Abimelech told Isaac that he should move away as he had become too powerful for them. Isaac obeyed and camped in the Valley of Gerar and settled there. Whilst Isaac was there, he reopened the wells that had been dug in the time of his father and which had been sealed up after Abraham died. He assigned them the same names Abraham had previously named them.

Meanwhile, Abimelech paid him a visit. When Isaac inquired as to the purpose of the visit, the king told him that they saw that the Lord was clearly with Isaac and they thought it would be best to have a sworn agreement between them. He suggested to Isaac that they make a treaty that neither of them would molest nor harm the other. They agreed and after Isaac had prepared a feast for them and they ate, the king and his men departed from the Valley of Gerar and left Isaac to continue to settle in the valley.

JACOB RECEIVES ISAAC'S BLESSING

When Isaac was old and his eyes were so weak that he could no longer see, he called for Esau, his older son and said to him, "My son, I am now an old man and don't know the day of my death. Now then, get your weapons—your quiver and bow—and go out to the open country to hunt some wild game for me. Prepare me the kind of tasty food I like and bring it to me to eat, so that I may give you my blessing before I die."

A blessing was also historically the way a family indicated who would become the head of the family when the father died. As with the birthright, it was usually given to the firstborn but there have been exceptions to this tradition. Genesis chapter 48 demonstrates a similar situation, where Jacob gives Joseph's younger son, Ephraim, his blessing instead of Manasseh (the eldest son); and Genesis chapter 49, where Jacob does not give Reuben (his firstborn by his wife, Leah), such a blessing but gave it to Joseph (his penultimate child, albeit his firstborn by his beloved Rachel), instead.

Now Rebekah was listening whilst Isaac spoke to his son, Esau. When Esau left for the open country to hunt game to bring back to his father, Rebekah called Jacob and said, "Look, I overheard your father saying to Esau that he must prepare for him a tasty meal so that he may bless him before he dies." Rebekah told Jacob to go out to the flock and bring her two choice young goats and she would prepare them just the way his father liked them so that he may give him (Jacob), his blessing (instead of Esau) before he died.

Jacob said to Rebekah, his mother, "But my brother Esau is a hairy man, and I'm a man with smooth skin. What if my father touches me? He would then think I am tricking him and would bring a curse on me instead of a blessing." But Rebekah said to her son, "Let the curse fall on me but just do as I asked and go and get the young goats for me." So Jacob did as his mother requested and Rebekah prepared some tasty food just the way Isaac liked it. Then she took the best clothes of Esau and she put them on Jacob. She also covered Jacob's hands and the smooth part of his neck with the goatskins. Then she handed Jacob the tasty food and the bread she had made and he went to his father.

When Jacob went to Isaac, Isaac was surprised that Esau could find game so quickly, but Jacob told his father that the Lord gave him success. Isaac then asked him to come near so that he could touch him, so that he could know if he was really his son, Esau and so Jacob did as his father asked. Isaac touched him and said, "The voice is the voice of Jacob but the hands are the hands of Esau." Jacob asked, "Are you really my son Esau?" Jacob replied, "I am." So Isaac asked him to bring him some of his game so that he could eat and give him his blessing.

After Isaac had eaten and drunk, he called his son closer so that he could kiss him and when Isaac caught the smell of his clothes he blessed him and said:

"Ah, the smell of my son is like the smell of a field that the Lord has blessed. May God give you of heaven's due and of earth's richness—an abundance of grain and new wine. May nations serve you and peoples bow down to you. Be lord over your brothers and may the sons of your mother bow down to you. May those who curse you be cursed and those who bless you be blessed."

As soon as Isaac finished blessing Jacob and he had left his presence, Esau came in from hunting, having prepared tasty food for his father. Esau asked his father to sit up and eat some of his game so that he may give him his blessing. But Isaac asked him, "Who are you?" Esau replied, "Your firstborn Esau." Isaac trembled violently and asked, "Who was it then that hunted game and brought it to me? I ate it just before you came in and I blessed him—and indeed he will be blessed!" When Esau heard his father's words, he burst out with a loud and bitter cry and said to his father, "Bless me too, my father!" Isaac said, "Your brother came deceitfully and took your blessing." Esau said, "Isn't he rightly named Jacob? He has deceived me twice: He took my birthright and now he's taken my blessing."

Esau continued to plead with his father to bless him but Isaac told him that he had made Jacob lord over him and had made all Jacob's relatives, including Esau his servants. He told him that Jacob will be sustained with grain and new wine. Isaac told Esau that he was not sure what he could possibly do for him now. But Esau pleaded, "Do you have only one blessing, my father? Bless me too, my father!" and Esau wept aloud.

Isaac answered Esau and told him that his dwelling place would be away from the earth's richness, away from the dew of the Heaven above. He told him that he would live by the sword and he would serve his brother, but that when he grew restless, he would throw his brother's yoke from his neck. So Esau held a grudge against Jacob and decided that once Isaac had died and they had finished mourning for him, he would kill Jacob. But when Rebekah found out Esau's plans, she told Jacob and sent him to Laban (her brother) in Haran for his own safety until Esau's fury subsided. So Jacob fled to stay with Laban in Haran.

On his way to Haran, Jacob had a dream at Bethel, during which God renewed the covenant with Jacob (to bless him and all peoples on earth through him; that his descendants would be like the dust of the earth and that he would possess Canaan), that He had made with his father, Isaac and his grandfather, Abraham. When Jacob awakened, he exclaimed, "Surely the Lord is in this place, and I was not aware of it. How awesome is this place! This is none other than the house of God; this is the gate of heaven."

He took the stone he had used as a pillow and set it up as a pillar and poured oil on top of it. He called the place Bethel and there made a vow to God saying, "If God will be with me and will watch over me on this journey and if I return safely to my father's house, then the Lord will be my God and this stone that I have set up as a pillar will be God's house and of all that you give me, I will give you a tenth."

JACOB PROVES HIS LOVE FOR RACHEL
(*An Example of True Love*)

As Jacob came near to Haran, he questioned some men he saw as to whether they knew Laban. They told him that they did know Laban and they showed him Laban's daughter, Rachel who was tending sheep, as she was a shepherdess. When Jacob saw Rachel, he went over to her, kissed her and wept aloud. He told her who he was and she ran and told her father. When Laban heard the news of Jacob he ran to meet him, embraced him, kissed him and brought him to his house.

So Jacob lived with Laban and worked for him. After about a month of working, Jacob asked him what his wages would be and he told Laban that he would work for seven years for the hand of his youngest daughter, Rachel. Rachel was lovely in form and beautiful and Jacob had fallen in love with her. Laban agreed, so Jacob worked seven years to get Rachel but to him it seemed only a few days because of his love for her.

At the end of the seven years, Jacob asked for the hand of his promised wife in marriage but Laban arranged a great feast and gave Jacob Leah (his eldest daughter) to marry instead of Rachel. When Jacob enquired as to why Laban had deceived him, Laban told him that it was not the custom in that land to give the youngest daughter's hand in marriage before the older one. He told him to marry Leah and finish the bridal week with her. Then they would give him Rachel to marry also, in return for another seven years of work (**as it was legal for a man to have more than one wife, as it still is in some countries in the world**). And Jacob did so, for he loved Rachel more than Leah. Then Laban gave Jacob Rachel to be his wife also.

THE CHILDREN OF JACOB
(11 of the 12 Tribes of Israel)

Now Jacob loved Rachel more than Leah and when the Lord saw that Leah was not loved, He opened up Leah's womb but Rachel was barren.

Leah became pregnant and gave birth to a son. She called him **Reuben**, for she said, "It is because the Lord has seen my misery. Surely my husband will love me now."

She conceived again and when she gave birth to a son, she said, "Because the Lord heard that I am not loved, he gave me this son too." So she named him **Simeon**.

Again she conceived, and when she gave birth to a son she said, "Now at last my husband will become attached to me, because I have borne him three sons." So he was named **Levi**.

She conceived again, and when she gave birth to a son, she said, "This time I will praise the Lord." So she named him **Judah**. After the birth of Judah, Leah stopped having children.

Meanwhile, when Rachel saw that she was not bearing Jacob any children, she became jealous of her sister and began to pressure Jacob to give her children but Jacob responded that he was not God, who had kept her from having children. So Rachel used her handmaid, Bilhah (**as a surrogate of sorts)** so that through Bilhah she could give her husband children. When Bilhah bore Jacob a son, Rachel said, "God has vindicated me; he has listened to my plea and has given me a son." Because of this, she named him **Dan**.

Rachel's servant, Bilhah conceived again and bore Jacob a second son. Then Rachel said, "I have had a great struggle with my sister, and I have won." So she named him **Naphtali**.

When Leah saw that she stopped having children, she too used her handmaid, Zilpah as a surrogate so that she could continue to give her husband children. Leah's servant bore Jacob a son. Then Leah said, "What good fortune!" So she named him **Gad**. Then the servant bore Jacob a second son. Then Leah said, "How happy I am! The women will call me happy!" So she named him **Asher**.

Then God opened up Leah's womb again and she became pregnant and bore Jacob a fifth son, whom she named **Issachar**, as she said that God had rewarded her for giving her handmaid to her husband. She conceived again and bore Jacob a sixth son to which she said, "God has presented me with a precious gift. This time my husband will treat me with honour because I have borne him six sons." So she named him **Zebulun**. Sometime later she gave birth to a daughter and named her Dinah.

Then God remembered Rachel. He listened to her and opened up her womb. She became pregnant and gave birth to a son and said, "God has taken away my disgrace." She named him **Joseph**, and said, "May the Lord add to me another son."

JACOB FLEES FROM LABAN

Jacob continued to work for Laban for a while and Jacob's flocks began to increase. His wives had also borne him children and after Rachel gave birth to Joseph, he was ready to leave Laban so that he could make a life for himself and his family. But Laban discouraged him from leaving. Jacob worked out an arrangement with Laban so that he could be paid with the speckled, spotted and dark-coloured lambs or goats (as these were the least of the flock). Laban agreed.

Jacob continued to tend Laban's flocks but also began to raise his own flocks (from the payment of flocks he received for tending to those of Laban). Over time, due to the method Jacob used for breeding the flock, Jacob grew exceedingly prosperous and came to own large flocks and maidservants and menservants and camels and donkeys. Laban became jealous of how wealthy Jacob had become and Jacob noticed that Laban had a different attitude toward him. Jacob also learnt that Laban's sons were saying that he had taken everything their father owned and had gained all his glory (wealth) from what belonged to their father. So the Lord said to Jacob, "Go back to the land of your fathers and to your relatives, and I will be with you." So Jacob, having explained the situation to his wives and having obtained his wives agreement (following which, Rachel stole her father's household gods whilst he was out shearing his sheep), left with his wives, children, servants and flocks, unknown to Laban.

When Laban learnt that Jacob had left, he pursued him and questioned his reason for leaving like a thief in the night without allowing him to kiss his daughters and his grandchildren goodbye. Jacob told him that he was afraid that if he knew he was leaving he would have taken his daughters from him by force. Laban could not harm Jacob however, as the Lord had already warned him in a dream against saying anything to Jacob whether good or bad.

After the two had sorted out their differences, they made a covenant that Jacob would not mistreat his daughters or take any other wife besides Laban's daughters, and that neither of them would bring harm to the other. Jacob then offered a sacrifice and they ate and slept. Early the next morning, Laban kissed his grandchildren and his daughters, blessed them, and returned home.

JACOB AND ESAU REUNITE AND THE TWELFTH TRIBE OF ISRAEL IS BORN

Jacob Prepares to Meet Esau

As God commanded Jacob to return to his relatives, Jacob began to prepare to meet Esau, whose wrath he had fled from when he went to live with Laban. So Jacob sent messengers ahead of him to Esau to let Esau know that he was coming home. He told his servants to let Esau know that his (Esau's) servant, Jacob, had cattle, donkeys, sheep, goats, menservants and maidservants. When the men returned to Jacob, they told Jacob that Esau was coming to meet him and four hundred men were with him.

Jacob was scared that Esau might be coming to seek revenge and so Jacob prayed to the Lord for protection. He then selected a gift for his brother from the flock. The gift consisted of two hundred female goats and twenty male goats, two hundred ewes and twenty rams, thirty female camels with their young, forty cows and ten bulls, and twenty female donkeys and ten male donkeys. He then instructed one of his servants, who went ahead of him, that when Esau asked to whom they belonged and where they were going with the animals, he was to say, "They belong to your servant Jacob. They are a gift sent to my lord Esau, and Jacob is coming behind us."

Jacob spent the night in the camp and did not meet Esau that night. Whilst he was alone, a man wrestled with him until daybreak but the man could not overpower him. When the man saw that he could not overpower him, he touched the socket of Jacob's hip so that Jacob's hip was wrenched as he wrestled with the man. When the man asked to be let go, Jacob replied, "I will not let you go until you bless me." So the man said, "Your name will no longer be Jacob. It will be Israel, because you have struggled with God and with men and have overcome." Jacob asked the man his name. The man did not tell him but he blessed Jacob there. So Jacob called the place Peniel, saying, "It is because I saw God face to face, and yet my life was spared." To this day, the Israelites do not eat the tendon attached to the socket of the hip, because the socket of Jacob's hip was touched near the tendon.

Jacob and Esau Meet

When Jacob looked up and saw Esau coming with his four hundred men, he divided the children amongst Leah, Rachel and the two maidservants. The maidservants were in the front, Leah and her children next and Rachel and Joseph in the rear. Jacob went ahead of them and bowed down to the ground seven times as he approached Esau. But Esau ran to meet Jacob and embraced him. He threw his arms around his neck and kissed him and they both wept.

Jacob then introduced his brother to his wives and children and offered Esau a portion of his flock as a gift. But Esau refused the gift saying to his brother that he (Esau) had plenty and that he (Jacob) should keep what he had for himself. So on that day, they both reunited as Esau had forgiven Jacob for taking his blessings all those years ago and Esau welcomed his brother home.

Once Jacob had arrived safely at the city of Shechem in Canaan, he bought a piece of land for a hundred pieces of silver and there he set up an altar and called it El Elohe Israel.

Rachel Dies after the Twelfth Tribe of Israel is Born

Following the reunion between Esau and Jacob, the Lord commanded Jacob to go up to Bethel and build him an altar there and Jacob did so. After moving past Bethel, Rachel who had conceived again, began to give birth but had great difficulty. The midwife said to her, "Don't be afraid, for you have another son." And as she breathed her last breath, for she died in childbirth, she named him Ben-Oni but his father named him **Benjamin**. The birth of Benjamin completed the twelve sons of Jacob (Israel), who would become known as the twelve tribes of Israel. Rachel was buried and over her tomb Jacob set up a pillar, and to this day that pillar marks Rachel's tomb in Bethlehem.

DINAH AND THE SHECHEMITES

Dinah, the daughter of Leah, whom she had borne to Jacob (and who was his only daughter), went out to visit the women of the land. When Shechem, the son of Hamor, the Hivite, the ruler of that area saw her, he took her and violated her (he forced her to have pre-marital sexual intercourse with him). His heart was drawn to Dinah; he loved her and spoke tenderly to her. He told his father that he wanted his help to get Dinah as his wife. When Jacob heard about what had happened to Dinah, her brothers were in the field so he kept quiet about it until they returned home.

Shechem's father went to speak to Jacob, but when her brothers came home, having heard what had happened, they were filled with grief and fury because Shechem had done a disgraceful thing in Israel by lying with Jacob's daughter— a thing that should not be done. Hamor told them that his son, Shechem had his heart set on Dinah and he asked that they would please give him Dinah for his son to wife. Hamor said, "Intermarry with us; give us your daughters and take our daughters for yourselves. You can settle among us; the land is open to you. Live in it, trade in it, and acquire property in it."

Shechem told Jacob and Dinah's brothers that he would do whatever they asked in order to find favour in their eyes. He said, "Make the price for the bride and the gift I am to bring as great as you like, and I'll pay whatever you ask me. Only give me the girl as my wife." The brothers responded deceitfully as they were upset that Dinah had been defiled.

They told Hamor that in order for Dinah to become the wife of his son, all the males amongst his people had to be circumcised. If this was done, then there could be intermarriage and then the Israelites could settle amongst his people. Hamor and Shechem agreed and all the men in the city were circumcised. Three days later and whilst all the men were still in pain, two of Jacob's sons, Simeon and Levi, Dinah's brothers, took their swords and attacked the unsuspecting city, killing every male. They killed Hamor and Shechem and took Dinah and left. They seized their flocks and herds and donkeys and everything else of theirs in the city and out in the fields. They carried off all their wealth and all their women and children, taking as plunder everything in the houses.

Then Jacob said to Simeon and Levi, "You have brought trouble on me by making me a stench to the Canaanites and Perizzites, the people living in this land. We are a few in number, and if they join forces against me and attack me, I and my household will be destroyed." But they replied, "Should he have treated our sister like a prostitute?"

JOSEPH SEES THE FUTURE THROUGH DREAMS

Joseph's Dreams

Israel (whose name God changed from Jacob), Joseph's father, lived in the land of Canaan together with his children. Joseph, a young man of seventeen tended his father's flocks together with his brothers. Israel loved Joseph more than any of his other sons, because he had been born to him in his old age (by Rachel, whom he loved); and he made a robe for him which was full of ornaments and many colours. When the brothers saw that their father loved him more than any of them, they hated him and could not speak a kind word to him.

At around the same time, Joseph had a dream and when he told it to his brothers, they hated him all the more. He said to them, "Listen to this dream I had: We were out working in the field gathering bundles of grain when suddenly my bundle arose and stood upright whilst your bundle gathered around mine and bowed down to it." His brothers said to him, "Do you intend to reign over us? Will you actually rule us?" And they hated him more because of this dream and what he had told them.

Then he had another dream and he told it to his brothers, "Listen, I had another dream, and this time the sun and moon and eleven stars were bowing down to me." When he told his father as well as his brothers, his father rebuked him and said, "What is this dream you had? Will your mother and I and your brothers actually come and bow down to the ground before you?" His brothers were jealous of him but his father pondered the matter in his mind.

Joseph Sold by His Brothers

One day, Joseph's brothers went to tend the sheep but Joseph stayed behind. So his father, Israel, sent Joseph to see how his brothers were getting on with the flocks so that Joseph could bring back word to him. Before he reached his brothers, they saw him in the distance and they plotted to kill him. They said, "Here comes that dreamer! Come now let us kill him and throw him into one of these cisterns and say that a ferocious animal devoured him. Then we'll see what comes of his dreams."

When Reuben heard this, he tried to rescue Joseph from their hands. "Let's not take his life," he said. "Don't shed any blood. Throw him into this cistern here in the desert but do not lay a hand on him." Reuben had said this to rescue Joseph from them at a later stage and take him back to his father. So they stripped Joseph of his richly ornamented robe and they threw him in the cistern (which was empty as it had no water in it). However, shortly thereafter, some Ishmaelites were passing on their way to Egypt and Judah convinced his other brothers that they would gain nothing to kill Joseph, after all he was their flesh and blood and that they should sell him to the Ishmaelites instead. The brothers agreed and they sold him to the Ishmaelites for twenty shekels of silver and the Ishmaelites took Joseph with them to Egypt.

When Reuben returned to the cistern to pull Joseph out, he saw that Joseph was not there and he was very saddened. He questioned his brothers about Joseph. Then they took Joseph's robe and dipped it in some blood of a goat they had slaughtered. They took the robe back to Israel and asked him to examine it to see if it was Joseph's. Israel recognised the robe to be Joseph's and concluded that a ferocious animal must have devoured him. Then Israel mourned for his son for many days. All his children came to comfort him but he refused to be comforted. He told them that he would go to the grave in mourning for his son and he wept for Joseph. Meanwhile, the Ishmaelites sold Joseph in Egypt to Potiphar, one of Pharaoh's officials— the captain of the guard. **As you may know, a Pharaoh was the name given to a king of Egypt in biblical times.**

JUDAH AND TAMAR

Judah left his brothers and went down to stay with a man of Adullam named Hirah. There he met the daughter of a Canaanite woman named Shuaa. He married her and she bore him three sons, Er, Onan and Shelah. Judah found a wife for Er, his firstborn. Her name was Tamar, but Er was wicked in the site of God so God put him to death at a young age. Then Judah told Onan that he had to make his brother's wife his wife, as he had a duty to her (as a brother-in-law) to produce an offspring for his brother. But Onan knew that the offspring would not be his so whenever he lay with his brother's wife, he spilled his semen on the ground to ensure that he did not get her pregnant. This was wicked in God's sight, so Onan was put to death at an early age also.

Judah then told Tamar to live with her father until his youngest son, Shelah grew up. But Judah thought that that son would die too, so he did not give Tamar to Shelah as his wife. One day, Judah was travelling to Timnah, the town where Tamar was living in her father's house, and Tamar knew, so she took off her widow clothes and disguised herself. When he saw her, he thought she was a prostitute and he asked her to sleep with him. She agreed to do so for a young goat from his flock, provided that he allowed her to keep his seal, its cord and the staff in his hand as a pledge until he sent back the young goat. When they slept together, she became pregnant by him.

When Judah sent back the young goat by his friend the Adullahmite, in order to get his pledge back from the woman he had slept with, she could not be found and he was informed that there was not a prostitute in that area. Judah then told his friend that they should let her keep what she had received, lest they became a laughing stock. About three months later, Judah was told that his daughter-in-law Tamar was found guilty of prostitution and that she became pregnant as a result. Judah instructed the men to bring her out and have her burned to death.

As she was being brought out, she sent a message to her father-in-law. "I am pregnant for the man who owns these," she said. And she added, "See if you recognise whose seal, cord and staff these are." Judah recognised them and said, "She is more righteous than I, since I wouldn't give her my son Shelah." And Judah did not sleep with her again.

When the time came for her to give birth, there were twin boys in her womb. As she was giving birth, one of them put out his hand; so the midwife took a scarlet thread and tied it on his wrist and said, "This one came out first." But when he drew back his hand, his brother came out, and she said, "So this is how you have broken out!" And he was named Perez (**and would be the one amongst the children of Israel, through whose bloodline Jesus, the Messiah would come**). Then his brother, who had the scarlet thread on his wrist, came out and he was given the name Zerah.

JOSEPH AND POTIPHAR'S WIFE

Joseph's Success in Egypt
Joseph was sold to one of Pharaoh's (the king of Egypt) top officials, the captain of Pharaoh's guard. The Lord was with Joseph in Egypt and he prospered, and he lived in the house of his Egyptian master. When his master saw that the Lord was with him and that the Lord gave him success in everything he did, Joseph found favour in his eyes and became his attendant. Potiphar put him in charge of his household and he trusted Joseph to care for everything that he owned. The blessings of the Lord were on everything in Potiphar's household because of Joseph.

Potiphar's Wife
Joseph was well-built and handsome and after a while his master's wife took notice of him and tried to get Joseph to pay attention to her and to sleep with her. Joseph refused. He said to her, "With me in charge, my master does not concern himself with anything in the house; everything he owns, he has entrusted to my care. No one is greater in this house than I am. My master has withheld nothing from me except you for you are his wife. How then could I do such a wicked thing and sin against God?" So Joseph avoided his master's wife day after day, no matter how much she tried to get his attention. Potiphar's wife grew angry at Joseph, lied on him and accused him of trying to rape her. When Potiphar heard it, he was very angry and sent Joseph to prison. But whilst Joseph was in prison, the Lord was with him and showed him kindness, so he granted him favour in the eyes of the prison warden. The warden put Joseph in charge of all that was done in the prison and paid no attention to anything under Joseph's care, because the Lord was with Joseph and gave him success in whatever he did.

JOSEPH INTERPRETS DREAMS

The Cupbearer and the Baker

Whilst Joseph was in prison, Pharaoh (king of Egypt) became angry with his chief cupbearer and chief baker and sent them to prison. The captain of the guard assigned them to Joseph and he attended to them. One night, and on the same night, both these men had two separate dreams. When Joseph came to see them the next morning, they both looked dejected so he asked them what was wrong. They told him they both had dreams the night before but that there was no one to interpret the dreams. Joseph questioned them as to whether interpretations did not belong to God. However, he then asked each of them to tell him their dreams.

The Cupbearer's Dream

The chief cupbearer told Joseph his dream. He said, "In my dream, I saw a vine in front of me, and on the vine there were three branches. As soon as it budded, it blossomed, and its clusters ripened into grapes. Pharaoh's cup was in my hand, and I took the grapes, squeezed them into Pharaoh's cup and put it in his hand." "This is what it means," Joseph said to him. "The three branches are three days. Within three days, Pharaoh will lift up your head and restore you to your position and you will put Pharaoh's cup in his hand, just as you used to do when you were his cupbearer." Joseph told him that when all begun to go well with him, he should remember him (Joseph) and show him kindness and that he should mention him to Pharaoh and get him out of the prison. Joseph said, "I was forcibly carried off from the land of the Hebrews, and even here, I have done nothing to deserve to be put in a dungeon."

The Baker's Dream

The baker was next. When the baker realised Joseph had given a favourable interpretation to the cupbearer, he said to Joseph, "I too had a dream: On my head were three baskets of bread. In the top baskets were all kinds of baked goods for Pharaoh, but the birds were eating them out of the baskets on my head." "This is what it means," Joseph said. "The three baskets are three days. Within three days Pharaoh will lift off your head and hang you on a tree. And the birds will eat away your flesh."

Now the third day was Pharaoh's birthday, and he gave a feast for all his officials. He lifted up the heads of the chief cupbearer and the chief baker in the presence of his officials. As Joseph had indicated, he restored the chief cupbearer to his position, but hanged the chief baker. However, the chief cupbearer did not remember Joseph as he had promised. He forgot him, so Joseph remained in prison.

JOSEPH INTERPRETS PHARAOH'S DREAMS

After about two full years following Joseph's interpretations of the dreams of the cupbearer and the baker whilst they were in prison, Pharaoh (king of Egypt) himself had two dreams in one night.

Pharaoh's First Dream

Pharaoh was standing by the Nile, when out of the river there came seven cows, sleek and fat and they grazed amongst the reeds. After these seven, another seven cows came up out of the Nile, but these were ugly and gaunt and they ate up the seven sleek, fat cows. After the dream, Pharaoh woke up.

Pharaoh's Second Dream

Pharaoh fell asleep again and had a second dream: Seven heads of grain, healthy and good, were growing on a single stalk. After these seven grains, seven other heads of grain sprouted. They were thin and scorched by the wind. The thin heads of grain swallowed up the seven healthy, full heads. Then Pharaoh woke up. When he woke up, he was troubled and sent for all the magicians and wise men of Egypt but no one could interpret the dreams for him.

The Cupbearer Tells Pharaoh of Joseph

The cupbearer was reminded of his shortcomings and told Pharaoh that Joseph had interpreted his dream and the chief baker's dream whilst they were both in prison and that exactly as Joseph had interpreted it, things happened—he was restored to his position and the chief baker was hanged. So Pharaoh sent for Joseph.

Joseph Meets Pharaoh

Joseph was brought before Pharaoh and Pharaoh told him his dreams. Joseph said, "I cannot interpret them, but God will give Pharaoh the answer he desires." He told Pharaoh that both his dreams were one and the same. That God had revealed to Pharaoh what He was about to do. The seven good cows represented seven years, and the seven good heads of grain also represented seven years. They both represented seven years of great abundance in Egypt. The seven lean, ugly cows that came up after also represented seven years and so did the seven worthless heads of grain scorched by the east wind: They represented seven years of famine which would follow the seven years of abundance. The seven years of abundance would not be remembered because the seven years of famine would be so severe. Joseph also told Pharaoh that the reason the dream was given to Pharaoh in two forms was that the matter had been firmly decided and that God would do it soon.

Joseph Instructs Pharaoh as the Lord Instructed Him
Joseph told Pharaoh that he needed to look for a discerning and wise man and that that man should be put in charge of the land of Egypt. He also told Pharaoh that commissioners would need to be appointed over the land; that they would need to take a fifth of the harvest of Egypt during the seven years of abundance and store up the grain in reserve for the country to be used during the seven years of famine that would come upon Egypt. Joseph indicated that if this was done, the country would not be ruined by the famine.

Pharaoh Chooses Joseph
When Pharaoh asked Joseph, "Where can we find anyone like this man, one in whom dwells the Spirit of God?" Pharaoh answered his own question and said to Joseph, "Since God has made all this known to you, there is no one as discerning and wise as you. You shall be in charge of my palace, and all my people are to submit to your orders. Only with respect to the throne, will I be greater than you."

Seven Years of Abundance

Pharaoh said to Joseph, "I hereby put you in charge of the whole land of Egypt." Then Pharaoh took his signet ring from his finger and put it on Joseph's finger. He dressed Joseph in robes of fine linen and put a gold chain around Joseph's neck. Joseph rode in a chariot as Pharaoh's second in command and men shouted before him, "Make way!" Pharaoh said to him, "I am Pharaoh, but without your word, no one will lift a hand or foot in all of Egypt." He gave Joseph the name Zaphenath-Paneah. He also gave him as a wife, the daughter of Potiphera, priest of On. Her name was Asenath.

Joseph in Charge of Egypt

Joseph was about thirty years old (**thirteen years after he had the dream**) when he entered the service of Pharaoh, king of Egypt. He was the Governor of the land. He went all about Egypt and during the years of abundance, he stored up huge quantities of grain, like the sand of the sea. It was so much that he stopped keeping records because it was beyond measure.

Joseph's Sons

During the years of abundance, two sons were born to Joseph by his wife. Joseph named his firstborn Manasseh and said, "It is because God has made me forget all my trouble and my father's entire household." The second son he named Ephraim and said, "It is because God has made me fruitful in the land of my suffering."

Seven Years of Famine

The seven years of abundance in Egypt came to an end, and the seven years of famine began, just as Joseph had indicated. There was famine in all the other surrounding lands, but in the entire land of Egypt, there was food. When all of Egypt began to feel the famine, the people cried to Pharaoh for food but Pharaoh sent them to Joseph and told them to do whatever Joseph told them to do.

When the famine had spread across the whole country, Joseph opened the store-houses and sold grain to the Egyptians, for the famine was severe throughout Egypt. And all the countries came to Egypt to buy grain from Joseph, because the famine was also severe in the entire world.

When Joseph collected all the monies that people had to buy grain, he then traded them grain for their livestock. When they had traded all their livestock, they agreed to trade their lands and then their service (to be in bondage to Pharaoh) in order to be able to survive. So Pharaoh owned all the lands in Egypt in return for providing food to the people during the famine years. Joseph commanded them to give one-fifth of their crops to Pharaoh whenever they planted seed and their crops came in.

Joseph therefore established it as a law concerning Egypt— still in force today—that one-fifth of the produce belonged to Pharaoh. It was only the land of the priest that did not become Pharaoh's (as the priests received a regular allotment from Pharaoh and had food enough from the allotment Pharaoh had given to them. They therefore did not need to sell their land when the famine grew most severe).

TEN TRIBES OF ISRAEL GO TO EGYPT

Joseph's Brothers Go to Egypt
When Israel (whose name was changed from Jacob to Israel) learnt that there was grain in Egypt, he sent ten of his sons to Egypt to buy grain. He did not send Benjamin, his last son by Rachel and Joseph's full-blood brother (by both mother and father), as he was afraid that harm might come to him.

Joseph's Dream About His Brothers Comes True
Joseph was the Governor of the land, the one who sold grain to all its people. So when Joseph's brothers arrived, they bowed down to him with their faces to the ground. They did not recognise Joseph but as soon as he saw them, he recognised them, yet pretended to be a stranger, and spoke harshly to them. He accused them of being spies.

They told him that there were twelve of them, one died and one is back home with their father, but Joseph still accused them of being spies. He told them that in order to prove their story, one of them must remain whilst the others went back to carry grain for their households but the youngest brother, Benjamin must be brought back to Egypt in order for them to prove that their word was true.

The brothers then remembered what they did to Joseph and communicated to one another aloud that they were being punished for what they did to him. They did not know that Joseph could understand them (as he spoke in Egyptian and was using an interpreter to speak to them). Joseph turned away from them and cried secretly and then turned back to them and spoke again. He took Simeon from them and bound him before their eyes.

Joseph's Brothers Go Back Home
Nine of the ten brothers that came returned home. Simeon was kept in Egypt by Joseph as a means to ensure that the brothers brought back Benjamin in order to prove that they were not spies. Joseph gave orders to fill their bags with grain, for them to be given provisions for their journey and for their silver to be returned to their sacks. On their way back, whilst stopping to rest for the night, they realised that their silver was in their sacks and they became very afraid and wondered what God had done to them. When they arrived back home, they told their father all that had happened and he too was frightened when he saw the silver he had given them to pay for the grain, returned in their sacks.

Israel Upset with His Sons
Israel said to them, "You have deprived me of my children. Joseph is no more and Simeon is no more, and now you want to take Benjamin. Everything is against me!" But Reuben assured his father that if he did not bring back Benjamin, he could put both of Reuben's sons to death. Israel was not convinced and he said, "My son will not go down there with you; his brother is dead and he is the only one left. If harm comes to him on the journey you are taking, you will bring my gray head down to the grave in sorrow."

Joseph's Brothers Visit Egypt Again!
The time came for more grain to be bought but the brothers reminded Israel that they could not go without Benjamin. Israel asked, "Why did you bring this trouble on me by telling the man you had another brother?" They replied, "The man questioned us closely about ourselves and our family. 'Is your father still living?' he asked us. 'Do you have another brother?' We simply answered his questions.

How were we to know he would say, 'Bring your brother down here'?"

Judah tried to assure Israel that he would take personal responsibility to bring Benjamin back, and eventually Israel agreed that if it must be done, it must be done. He told them to take some of the best produce of the land (honey, balm, pistachio nuts, almonds, spices and myrrh) to present to the man as a gift, and to take double the amount of silver they took on the first trip. He also told them to take back the silver that had mysteriously returned with them from the first trip as well. Israel said, "May God Almighty grant you mercy before the man so that he would let your other brother and Benjamin come back with you..."

Joseph Eats with His Brothers
When the ten tribes of Israel arrived in Egypt and Joseph saw Benjamin with them, he instructed the steward of his house to take the men to his (Joseph's) house; to slaughter an animal and to prepare dinner, as the men (his brothers) were to eat with him at noon. His brothers were frightened and thought it was because of the silver that they had found in their sacks when they were returning home on their first trip. So they explained the situation to Joseph's steward but the steward told them not to worry, that their God, the God of their father gave them treasure in their sacks. He then brought Simeon to them and prepared them for their meal.

When Joseph came, they presented him with the gifts and bowed down to him to pay him honour. He questioned them about Israel and they replied that he was alive and well. When Joseph saw Benjamin up close, he said, "God be gracious to you my son." And he hurried out of the room (so they would not see him) and looked for a place to weep. When he was able to control himself, he came back out and went to eat with his brothers. Joseph loved Benjamin, his mother's son and when portions were served to the brothers, Benjamin had five times as much as anyone else.

Joseph Plants Evidence against Benjamin

Joseph wanted Benjamin to stay with him for a while, whilst the other brothers went back, so he instructed his steward to place his silver cup in Benjamin's sack. When the brothers left, Joseph sent his steward to chase after them and asked them why they had stolen his silver cup. The brothers denied it but then the cup was found in Benjamin's sack after a search was done. Prior to the search, they had agreed with Joseph's servant that the person in whose sack the cup was found, would become Joseph's slave and the rest of them would be free from blame. However, as the silver was found in Benjamin's sack, the brothers then went back to see Joseph as they did not intend to go back to their father without Benjamin.

Judah spoke to Joseph on behalf of his brothers and begged him for pardon for Benjamin. He explained that Benjamin's brother, Joseph died, and Benjamin was the only one of his mother's sons left and that their father loved him dearly. Judah told Joseph that their father had already told them that if Benjamin was not returned, he would go to his grave in misery. Judah then asked Joseph to take him as a slave in the place of Benjamin as he could not go back to his father if Benjamin was not with him. Judah (**emphatically**) said, "No! Do not let me see the misery that would come upon my father."

Joseph Makes Himself Known to His Brothers

Joseph could no longer control himself before all his attendants and he cried out, "Have everyone leave my presence!" So he made himself known to his brothers and there was no one else with Joseph when he made himself known to his brothers. He wept so loudly that the Egyptians heard him, and Pharaoh's household heard about it. Joseph said to his brothers, "I am Joseph! Is my father still living?"

But his brothers were not able to answer him because they were terrified at his presence. He told them not to be angry with themselves for selling him to Egypt, as the Lord had sent him ahead of them in order to save lives by a great deliverance. He told them that two years of the famine had gone but that the famine would continue for another five years. He continued to try to convince them that it was God who sent him there and not them.

He told them that God had made him lord over all Egypt and that they should come with their families and all their possessions to live in Egypt with him. He asked them to tell his father of all the glory (honour and wealth) that was accorded him in Egypt and that they should bring his father quickly. Then he threw his hands around Benjamin and wept and Benjamin embraced him, weeping also. He then kissed all his brothers and wept over them. Afterwards, his brothers spoke with him.

Pharaoh Supports Joseph
When Pharaoh heard what had happened, Pharaoh and all his officials were pleased. Pharaoh told him that he would give him the best of the land for his brothers and their family so that he could enjoy the fat of the land. He also told Joseph to tell his brothers not to worry about bringing their belongings with them because the best of Egypt would belong to them. So the brothers left, with loaded donkeys filled with the best of Egypt. They were given carts for their children and their wives and were also given provisions for their journey. He gave them new clothing also, but to Benjamin he gave three hundred shekels and

five sets of clothes. Then he sent his brothers on their way and as they were leaving, he admonished them, "Don't quarrel on the way!"

Israel Learns that Joseph is Alive

The brothers arrived back to Canaan and told Israel all that had happened. They said, "Joseph is alive! In fact he is ruler of all Egypt." Israel was stunned; he did not believe them. But when they told him everything Joseph had said to them, and when he saw the carts Joseph sent to bring him to Egypt, the spirit of their father revived. And Israel said, "I am convinced! My son Joseph is still alive. I will go see him before I die."

Israel Goes to Egypt to See Joseph

So Israel set out with all that he had and when he reached Beersheba, he offered sacrifices to the God of his father, Isaac. God spoke to him in a vision at night and said, "Jacob! Jacob! I am God, the God of your father. Do not be afraid to go down to Egypt, for I will make you into a great nation there. I will go down to Egypt with you, and I will surely bring you back again. And Joseph's own hand will close your eyes."

When Joseph saw Israel, his father appearing, he had his chariot ready to meet him. As soon as Joseph appeared before his father, he threw his arms around his father and wept for a long time. Israel said to Joseph, "Now I am ready to die, since I have seen for myself that you are alive." Then Joseph took his father and brothers to meet Pharaoh. Israel was 130 years old when he was reunited with Joseph. He had not seen him in approximately seventeen years. Israel blessed Pharaoh and then went to settle in the land that Pharaoh had provided for them to settle in.

Joseph Makes a Promise to His Father
Israel lived in Egypt seventeen years and he lived to be 147
years old. When the time drew near for him to die, he
called for his son, Joseph and said to him, "If I have found
favour in your eyes, put your hand under my thigh and
promise that you will show me kindness and faithfulness.
Do not bury me in Egypt, but when I rest with my fathers,
carry me out of Egypt and bury me where they are buried."
Joseph agreed to do as his father asked but Israel said,
"Swear to me." Then Joseph swore to him that he would
bury him in the land of his fathers in the cave in the field of
Machpelah near Mamre where Abraham, Sarah, Isaac,
Rebekah and Leah were buried.

Israel Gives His Blessings Before He Dies
When Joseph learnt that his father was ill, he took his two
sons, Manasseh and Ephraim to see him. When Israel
heard that Joseph was there to see him, he rallied his
strength and sat up on the bed. He told Joseph that on his
way to Egypt the Lord appeared to him in a dream and
blessed him and that God told him that He would make him
fruitful and would increase his numbers. He would make
him a community of peoples and would give the land to
him as an everlasting possession and to his descendants
after him.

He told Joseph that the two sons he had in Egypt
(Manasseh and Ephraim) before he (Israel) came to see him
there, would be reckoned as his (Israel's), just as Reuben
and Simeon were his (Israel's). And that any children born
to him (Joseph) after those two would be Joseph's. He then
explained to him how his mother, Rachel had died, how
much it had saddened him and where she was buried.

When Israel saw the sons of Joseph, he asked for them to
come close to him so that he could bless them. He kissed

94

them and embraced them. He said to Joseph, "I never expected to see your face again, and now God has allowed me to see your children too." Then Joseph removed them from Israel's knees and bowed down his face to the ground and Joseph took both of them, Ephraim toward Israel's left hand and Manasseh on his right hand. Israel blessed both sons but gave Ephraim, the younger son, the blessing with his right hand. Joseph tried to correct him (as Israel's sight was failing him at his age). However, Israel assured Joseph that he knew who the elder was and who was the younger. He explained that whilst Manasseh, the firstborn, would become great, his younger brother would be greater than him and that his younger brother's descendants would become a group of nations.

He then said to Joseph, "I am about to die, but God will be with you and take you back to the land of your fathers. And to you, as one who is over your brothers, I give you the ridge of land I took from the Amorites with my sword and bow." Israel then called each of his sons so that he could bless them and tell them what would happen to them in the days to come.

Blessings on the Twelve Tribes of Israel
Reuben – was the firstborn, but because he defiled his father's bed by sleeping with one of his father's concubines, Israel told him that he would no longer excel.

Simeon and **Levi** – were also told that they would be scattered and dispersed in Israel because of their anger which they used to kill men and their cruelty which they used to hamstrung oxen as they pleased.

Judah – was told that he would be praised by his brothers and that his hand would be on the neck of his enemies. His father's sons would bow down to him. The scepter would not depart from him and the ruler's staff from between his feet.

Zebulun – was told that he would live by the seashore and become a haven for ships.

Issachar – was said by his father to be a strong ass lying down between two saddlebags and that when he saw how good his resting place (settled life), and how pleasant the land was, he would bend his shoulder to the burden (yield to it) and submit to forced labour.

Dan – was told that he would provide justice for his people as one of the tribes of Israel.

Gad – was told that he would be attacked but he would attack back at the heels.

Asher – was told that his food would be rich and that he would provide delicacies fit for a king.

Naphtali – was said to be a doe set free that bears beautiful fawns.

Joseph – was described as a fruitful vine; though he was attacked with bitterness and had been shot at with hostility, his bow remained steady and his strong arms stayed limber. God had helped him and the Almighty had blessed him with blessings of the heavens above, blessings of the deep that lies below, blessings of the breast and the womb. His father's blessings were greater than the blessings of ancient mountains, than the bounty of aged-old hills, "So let all these rest on the head of Joseph, on the brow of the prince among his brothers", Israel said.

Benjamin – was said to be a ravenous wolf, in the morning he devours prey and in the evening he divides the plunder.

So this was what their father, Israel said to them when he blessed them, giving each the blessing appropriate to him.

Joseph received the blessing that the firstborn (Simeon) would have normally received. The story also appears to illustrate that Joseph received a double portion of his father's blessings as he received his own blessing and his two sons received blessings from Israel (as if they were his (Israel's) sons) as well.

Israel's/Jacob's Death
After Jacob blessed his sons, he gave them these instructions: "I am about to be gathered to my people. Bury me with my fathers in the cave in the field of Ephron, the Hittite, the cave in the field of Machpelah, near Mamre in Canaan, which Abraham bought as a burial place from Ephron the Hittite, along with the field." He reminded them that Abraham and his wife, Sarah and Isaac and his wife, Rebekah were buried there and that he also buried Leah there. When he was finished instructing them, he drew up his feet into the bed, breathed his last breath and was gathered with his people.

Joseph threw himself on his father, wept over him and kissed him. He then directed the physicians in his service to embalm his father. The embalming took forty days (as this was the time required for embalming) and Egypt mourned him for seventy days. When the days of mourning were over, Joseph then went to Pharaoh, explained the promise he had made to his father and sought Pharaoh's permission to fulfill the promise to take his father back to Canaan to be buried. Pharaoh approved and said, "Go up and bury your father, as he made you swear to do." So Joseph and all the members of his household, his brothers and all the members of Jacob's household made the journey to Canaan. Only their children, their flocks and herds were left in Goshen. They were accompanied by all Pharaoh's officials—the dignitaries of Pharaoh's court and all the dignitaries in Egypt. Chariots and horsemen also went up with them. It was a gargantuan (very large) delegation.

On their way to Canaan, when they reached the threshing floor of Atad, near the Jordan, they cried and lamented bitterly over Jacob and Joseph observed a seven-day period of mourning for his father. When the Canaanites who lived there saw the mourning at the threshing floor, they discussed amongst themselves that the Egyptians were holding a solemn ceremony of mourning and this is why the place near the Jordan is called Abel Mizra-im.

So Jacob's sons did as he had commanded them. They carried him to the land of Canaan and buried him in the cave in the field of Machpelah, near Mamre, which Abraham had brought from Ephron, the Hittite as a burial place. After burying his father, Joseph returned to Egypt, together with his brothers and all the others who had gone with him.

Joseph Reassures His Brothers

When Joseph's brothers saw that their father was dead, they were afraid that Joseph might hold a grudge against them and pay them back for all the wrongs they did to him. So they sent word to Joseph indicating that his father had asked that he forgive them for their wrongs and their sins and when their message came to Joseph, he wept. His brothers then came to him and told him that they were his slaves.

But Joseph said to them, "Don't be afraid. Am I in the place of God? You intended to harm me, but God intended it for good to accomplish what is now being done, the saving of many lives. So then, don't be afraid. I will provide for you and your children." And he reassured them and spoke kindly to them.

Joseph's Death
Joseph lived until he was 110 years old and he remained in Egypt. He was able to see his great, great grandchildren by Ephraim and his great grandchildren by Manasseh. When he was about to die, he said to his brothers, "I am about to die. But God will surely come to your aid and take you up out of this land to the land he promised on oath to Abraham, Isaac and Jacob." And Joseph made the sons of Israel swear an oath and said, "God will surely come to your aid, and then you must carry my bones up from this place." So after he died, they embalmed him and he was placed in a coffin in Egypt.

STORIES OF EXODUS

An Exodus is a mass departure (involving large numbers of people) from one place to another. Exodus is the title given to the second book of the Bible and is also called the second book of Moses. It is therefore the second book of the Pentateuch. Exodus is derived from the root words "going out" and was given its name because the majority of the book is dedicated to the journey of the children of Israel out of Egypt. At the end of Genesis, the Israelites were welcomed visitors in Egypt due to the wisdom of Joseph. However, after the passage of hundreds of years, they had become slaves in Egypt following the emergence of a new Pharaoh who was not knowledgeable of the important role Joseph played in the history of Egypt. Exodus illustrates the beginning of God's manifestation of His covenant with Abraham as He begun to deliver His people out of bondage. It further illustrates the sufferings of the Israelites in Egypt, the mighty hand of God against Egypt when Pharaoh refused to let the Egyptians go, the orchestration of the departure, guidance during the departure from Egypt and the provision of the laws (the Ten Commandments) by God, pursuant to which Moses was to regulate the civil, social and religious life of the Israelites. It is a book which demonstrates God's persistence in delivering on His promise in removing His people out of bondage, even in circumstances where His assistance is not appreciated by the people. The teachings of Exodus are as applicable today as they were in biblical times and contain valuable instructions for children of God to adopt and follow as (applicable).

ISRAELITES OPPRESSED IN EGYPT

The Israelites are the descendants of Israel/Jacob who left Canaan to live in Egypt when there was a world famine. They had reconnected with Joseph who was the son of Israel and their brother, and who was the Governor of all of Egypt at the time. The descendants of Israel, including the twelve tribes and their families at the time they moved to Egypt were about seventy and Joseph was already in Egypt with his wife and two sons. When Joseph and all his brothers died, the Israelites continued to be fruitful; they multiplied greatly and became exceedingly numerous, so that the land was filled up with them.

Eventually however, the Pharaoh that ruled during Joseph's lifetime had died and a new king, who did not know about Joseph, came into power in Egypt. The new king was concerned with the rate at which the Israelites were multiplying. He thought that they had become too numerous and could be a real threat against the Egyptians if war should ever break out, as they could join the enemies of the Egyptians and fight against them. He therefore decided to deal harshly with them to prevent them from becoming more numerous and multiplying in their numbers.

The new Pharaoh therefore put slave masters over the Israelites to oppress them with forced labour. However, the more they were oppressed, the more they multiplied. The more they multiplied, the more they were feared by the Egyptians, so they worked them mercilessly. They made their lives bitter and hard with all kinds of work on and off the fields. In all the hard labour of the Israelites, the Egyptians handled them without regard or mercy.

When oppression was not enough, the king of Egypt commanded the Israelite midwives to kill every boy child of the Israelites that they helped to deliver from the Israelite women during childbirth. **A midwife is a person that is not a qualified doctor but skilled in the delivery of babies and offers support to pregnant women.** The midwives feared God however, and did not do what the king told them to do. They let the boys live. When they were asked by Pharaoh why they let the boys live, they told Pharaoh that the Israelite women were not like the Egyptian women. They indicated that Israelite women were very vigorous and would usually give birth before the midwife arrived. As a result, God was kind to the midwives and because the midwives feared the Lord in their actions, He gave them families of their own. So the Israelites continued to multiply and became even more numerous.

THE BIRTH AND EARLY LIFE OF MOSES

Pharaoh was still concerned about the increasing numbers of the Israelites, so he gave an order to all his people: "Every boy that is born, you must throw into the River Nile, but let every girl live." One of the descendants of Levi (Joseph's brother) married a Levite woman and she became pregnant and gave birth to a son. When she saw that the child was a fine child, she hid him for three months so that he would be spared from the order of the Pharaoh. When she could hide him no longer, she took a basket made from papyrus (a tall water plant) for him and coated it with tar and pitch. She then placed him in it and put the basket amongst the reeds along the bank of the River Nile. His sister, Miriam stood at a distance to see what would happen to him.

One day, Pharaoh's daughter went down to the Nile to bathe and her attendants were walking along the river bank. She saw the basket amongst the reeds and sent her slave girl to get it. When she opened it, she saw the baby inside. He was crying and she felt sorry for him. She recognised that he was one of the Israelite babies. The baby's sister, who was standing at a distance, asked Pharaoh's daughter, "Shall I go and get one of the Israelite women to nurse the baby for you?" "Yes, go," she answered. And the girl went and brought the baby's mother. Pharaoh's daughter said to the woman, "Take this baby and nurse him for me, and I will pay you." So the woman took the baby and nursed him (without Pharaoh's daughter's knowledge that she was actually his mother). When the child grew older, she took him to Pharaoh's daughter and he became her son. Pharaoh's daughter named him Moses, saying, "I drew him out of the water."

One day, after Moses had grown up, he went out to where the Israelites were and saw his own people at their hard labour. He witnessed an Egyptian beating an Israelite and thinking no one had seen him, he killed the Egyptian and buried him in the sand. Later he saw two Israelites fighting and when he asked the one in the wrong why he was fighting his fellowman, the man asked him who had made him judge over them and whether he was thinking on killing them the way in which he had killed the Egyptian. Moses then realised that what he did had become known and when Pharaoh learnt of it, he tried to kill Moses. Moses therefore fled from Pharaoh and went to live in Midian.

Whilst he was there, he was introduced to a Midian priest whose name was Jethro. Jethro had seven daughters. Moses agreed to stay with the priest and the priest gave Moses his daughter, Zipporah's hand in marriage and she bore him a son. During that period, the king of Egypt died and the Israelites groaned in their slavery and cried out for help. The Lord heard them and remembered His covenant with Abraham, Isaac and Jacob. So God looked upon the Israelites and was concerned about them.

GOD SPEAKS TO MOSES THROUGH
A BURNING BUSH

One day, Moses was tending the flock of Jethro, his father-in-law. He led the flock to the far side of the desert and came to Horeb, the mountain of God. Whilst he was there, the angel of the Lord appeared to him in flames of fire from within a bush. Moses thought it strange that the bush was on fire for some time and it did not burn up so he went over to see why the bush did not burn up. When God saw that Moses had gone over to look at the bush, God called him from within the bush, "Moses! Moses!" and Moses said, "Here I am."

God said to him, "Do not come any closer. Take off your sandals, for the place where you are standing is holy ground." Then the Lord said, "I am the God of your father, the God of Abraham, the God of Isaac and the God of Jacob. I have indeed seen the misery of my people in Egypt. I have heard them crying out because of their slave drivers and I am concerned about their suffering. So I have come down to rescue them from the land of the Egyptians and to bring them up out of that land into a good and spacious land, a land filled with milk and honey—the home (at the time) of the Canaanites, Hittites, Amorites, Perizzites, Hivites and Jebusites. And now the cry of the Israelites has reached me, and I have seen the way the Egyptians are oppressing them. So now go, I am sending you to Pharaoh to bring my people, the Israelites out of Egypt."

Moses Questions God's Choice of Him
Moses questioned whether he was the right person to be charged with that responsibility. He said, "Who am I, that I should go to Pharaoh and bring the Israelites out of Egypt?" And God said, "I will be with you. And this will be the

105

sign to you that it is I who have sent you: When you have brought the people out of Egypt, you will worship God on this mountain." Moses then said to God, "Suppose I go to the Israelites and say to them, 'The God of your fathers has sent me to you and they ask me, 'What is his name?' Then what shall I tell them?'" God then said to Moses, "I AM WHO I AM. This is what you say to the Israelites: 'I AM has sent me to you.'" God told him to tell the Israelites that the God of Abraham, Isaac and Jacob had sent him to them. He had told Moses to go and assemble the elders and tell them what He told him and that the elders would listen to him. Moses was commanded by God that he and the elders were to go to Egypt and tell the king that they had met with the Lord, the God of the Israelites. He warned them that the king of Egypt would not let them go unless a mighty hand compelled him. God told Moses that He would stretch out His hand and strike the Egyptians with all the wonders that He would perform amongst them and after that, Pharaoh would let them go. God also told him that the Egyptians would also favour the Israelites so that when they left Egypt, they would not leave empty-handed.

Signs for Moses
Moses asked God what he should do if the people did not believe him. The Lord then told him to throw the staff he had in his hand on the ground. When Moses threw it on the ground, it became a snake and he ran from it. Then the Lord told him to reach out his hand and grab the snake by the tail, so Moses did so and it turned back into a staff in his hand. The Lord said to him, "This is so that they may believe that the Lord, the God of their fathers—the God of Abraham, the God of Isaac and the God of Jacob—has appeared to you." Then the Lord said to Moses, "Put your hand inside your cloak." So Moses put his hand into his cloak, and when he took it out, it was leprous, white like snow. "Now put it back in," God said, and when he did

and took it back out it was restored like the rest of his flesh. Then the Lord said, "If they do not believe you or pay attention to the first miraculous sign, they may believe the second, but if they do not believe these two signs or listen to you, take some water from the Nile and pour it on dry ground. The water you take from the river will become blood on the ground."

Moses Continues to Question God's Choice of Him
But Moses still struggled with God, and said, "O Lord, I have never been eloquent, neither in the past nor since you have spoken to me. I am slow of speech and tongue." **Moses had a speech impediment and so it affected his self-confidence.** The Lord said to him, "Who gave man his mouth? Who makes him deaf or mute? Who gives him sight or makes him blind? Is it not I, the Lord? Now go; I will help you speak and teach you what to say." But Moses said, "O Lord, please send someone else to do it." Then the Lord became really angry with Moses and asked him, "What about your brother Aaron, the Levite? I know he can speak well. He is already on his way to meet you and his heart will be glad to see you. You shall speak to him and put words in his mouth. I will help both of you speak and will teach you what to do. He will speak to the people for you, and it will be as if he were your mouth and as if I were God to him. But take this staff in your hand so that you can perform miraculous signs with it."

MOSES RETURNS TO EGYPT

Moses went back to Jethro, his father-in-law and told him that he needed to go back to Egypt to see if any of his people were still alive. So Jethro agreed and wished him well. God assured Moses that he could go back to Egypt as all the men who had wished to kill him were dead. So he took his wife and sons and started back to Egypt. He had the staff of God in his hand. Whilst on his journey, God told Moses to perform all the wonders He gave him the power to perform in Pharaoh's presence. But God warned him that He would harden Pharaoh's heart so that he would not let the people go. Moses should then say to Pharaoh that Israel is God's firstborn and if he does not let Israel go so that they could worship Him, He would kill Pharaoh's firstborn also.

At a lodging place on the way, the Lord met Moses and was about to kill him. But Zipporah took a flint knife, cut off her son's foreskin and touched Moses' feet with it. "Surely, you are a bridegroom of blood to me," she said (referring to circumcision). So the Lord let him alone.

Then Aaron (who was sent by God to meet Moses in the desert) and Moses met in the desert at the mountain of God. Moses told Aaron everything the Lord had sent him to say, and all about the miraculous signs He had commanded him to perform. So Moses and Aaron gathered together all the elders of the Israelites and Aaron told them everything the Lord had said to Moses. He also performed the signs before the people and they believed. And when they heard that the Lord was concerned about them and had seen their misery, they bowed down and worshipped.

Pharaoh's Displeasure in Moses' Request
So Moses and Aaron went to Pharaoh and said, "This is what the Lord, the God of Israel, says: 'Let my people go, so that they may hold a festival to me in the desert.'" Pharaoh replied, "Who is the Lord that I should obey him and let Israel go? I do not know the Lord and I will not let Israel go." They told Pharaoh that if he did not let the Israelites journey to the desert to offer up sacrifices to their God, the Lord might strike them with plagues or with the sword.

But Pharaoh did not listen; instead, he increased the labour of the Israelites. He commanded his men not to provide straw for the Israelites to make bricks. They therefore had to find their own straw but still make the same number of bricks they made per day as they did when straw was provided to them. So they had to work much harder but in less time. When they could not fulfill their quota, they were beaten and were called lazy and Pharaoh multiplied their labour and their misery. The Israelites were displeased by this and blamed Moses and Aaron. They said, "May the Lord look upon you and judge you! You have made us a stench to Pharaoh and his officials and have put a sword in their hand to kill us."

God Promises Deliverance to the Israelites
Moses returned to the Lord and said, "O Lord, why have you brought trouble upon this people? Is this why you sent me? Ever since I went to Pharaoh to speak in your name, he has brought trouble upon this people, and you have not rescued your people at all." Then the Lord said to Moses, "Now you will see what I will do to Pharaoh: Because of my mighty hand he will let them go; because of my mighty hand he will drive them out of his country."

The Lord re-established His covenant with Moses that he had made with Abraham, Isaac and Jacob. He told Moses to remind the Israelites that He was their God and that He would bring them out from under the yoke of the Egyptians. He promised to free them from being slaves to the Egyptians; He promised to redeem them with an outstretched arm and with mighty acts of judgments; and He promised to bring them to the land He had promised their fathers before them. Moses reported this to the Israelites but they did not listen to him because of their discouragement and the cruel bondage Pharaoh had inflicted upon them.

SIGNS AND WONDERS IN EGYPT

Then the Lord said to Moses, "Go, tell Pharaoh, king of Egypt to let the Israelites go out of his country." But Moses said to the Lord, "If the Israelites will not listen to me, why would Pharaoh listen to me, since I speak with faltering lips?" The Lord said to him, "See, I have made you like God to Pharaoh, and your brother, Aaron will be your prophet. You are to say everything that I command you, and your brother Aaron is to tell Pharaoh to let the Israelites go out of his country." The Lord again warned them however, that, "Pharaoh will harden his heart and he will not listen to you although I multiply my miraculous signs and wonders. Then I will lay my hand on Egypt and my mighty acts of judgment will bring out my divisions, my people, the Israelites. And the Egyptians will know that I am the Lord when I stretch out my hand against Egypt and bring the Israelites out of it." So Moses and Aaron did as the Lord commanded. At the time they spoke to Pharaoh, Moses was eighty years old and Aaron was eighty-three.

Aaron's Staff Becomes a Snake
The Lord told Aaron and Moses that whenever the Lord commanded Aaron to perform a miracle, that he was to take his staff and throw it down before Pharaoh and it would become a snake. So Aaron went before Pharaoh and did as God commanded but Pharaoh also summoned his wise men and sorcerers, and the Egyptian magicians performed the same wonders Aaron performed by their secret arts: Each one threw down his staff and it became a snake, but Aaron's staff swallowed up their staffs. Yet Pharaoh's heart became hard and he would not listen to them just as the Lord had said.

111

The Plague of Blood

The Lord told Moses that Pharaoh was not going to let the Israelites go as his heart was hard against it, so he should go to Pharaoh in the morning whilst he was going out to the water and wait for him on the bank of the Nile. God told Moses that when Pharaoh arrived there, Moses was to tell Pharaoh that the Lord had asked him to let His people go and he had refused, and that God would send a plague to him so that when the water in Egypt was struck with the staff that Moses held in his hand, the water would change to blood; the fish in the Nile would die; the river would stink and the Egyptians would not be able to drink its water. The Lord told Moses that the staff was to be stretched out over all the waters of Egypt and once that was done, every canal, stream, pond and reservoir would be turned into blood and blood would be everywhere in Egypt, even in wooden buckets and stone jars.

Moses and Aaron did as the Lord commanded them and when Aaron raised his staff in the presence of Pharaoh, all the water turned to blood, the fish in the Nile died and the river smelled so bad that the Egyptians could not drink the water. Blood was everywhere in Egypt. But the Egyptian magicians did the same thing by their secret arts, so Pharaoh's heart became hard and he would not listen to Moses and Aaron, just as the Lord had said. He turned and went into his palace not taking the plague to heart. Meanwhile, all the Egyptians dug along the Nile to get drinking water, because they could not drink the water of the river.

The Plague of Frogs

Seven days passed after the Lord struck the Nile. Then the Lord said to Moses that he should speak to Pharaoh again and if Pharaoh did not let the Israelites go, the country would be plagued with frogs. The frogs would come up into the palace and into the bedrooms in the palace and into the houses of Pharaoh's officials and the houses of the people, even in the ovens and kneading troughs of the Egyptians. So Aaron stretched forth the staff over the water and the frogs appeared but the magicians did the same things by their secret arts and made frogs appear in Egypt. However, Pharaoh called Moses and Aaron and told them that if they took the frogs away from the Egyptians, he would let the Israelites go to make sacrifices to their God. Moses and Pharaoh agreed that the next day the frogs would leave the houses of the people but Moses confirmed to Pharaoh that the frogs in the Nile would remain.

Moses prayed to God to relieve the Egyptians of the frogs and God heard his prayer and the frogs died in the houses, the courtyards and the fields. But when Pharaoh saw that there was relief, he hardened his heart and would not listen to Moses.

The Plague of Gnats

So the Lord sent a plague of gnats upon Egypt and when Aaron struck the dust of the ground, the dust became gnats. All the dust throughout the land became gnats and the gnats were on men and animals. When the magicians tried to produce gnats by their secret arts, they could not. So the magicians said to Pharaoh, "This is the finger of God." But Pharaoh hardened his heart and still would not listen.

The Plague of Flies

The Lord instructed Moses that He would next send a plague of flies upon Pharaoh and his people. However, He would not extend the plague to Goshen, the place where the Israelites were living in Egypt, and He was doing this so that Pharaoh would know that the Lord was in the land. God intended to make a distinction between the Israelites and the Egyptians with the plague of flies. And the Lord did it and when the flies came, Pharaoh summoned Moses and Aaron and told them that the Israelites could make sacrifices to their God but they must do it in Egypt. Moses disagreed and reminded Pharaoh that the Egyptians greatly hated the Israelites' sacrifices and that the Egyptians would stone them if they saw the Israelites making the sacrifices to their God. So Pharaoh agreed that they could go in the desert but not very far. Moses then prayed for the flies to be removed and the Lord removed them. Not a fly was left. As soon as Pharaoh was relieved again, he hardened his heart and would not let the Israelites go.

The Plague on Livestock
The Lord sent a plague on the livestock of the Egyptians but not on the livestock of the Israelites. Every animal of the Egyptians died but not one of the livestock of the Israelites died. Pharaoh sent men to check on the Israelites livestock and found that they were alive but he still hardened his heart.

The Plague of Boils
The Lord then sent a plague of boils on the Egyptians. The magicians too, were plagued with boils and could not stand before Moses. But Pharaoh hardened his heart and still would not listen to Moses and Aaron.

The Plague of Hail
The Lord decided to send the worst hailstorm that had ever fallen on Egypt. He told Moses to command Pharaoh that his people should bring their livestock and everything they had in the field to a place of shelter because the hail would fall on every man and animal that had not been brought in and was still out in the field and they would die. Those Egyptians that feared the word of the Lord did as Moses instructed Pharaoh but those that did not, left their livestock

and slaves in the field. **It is assumed that some time must have elapsed between the plague on livestock in Exodus 9:1 (where all the Egyptian livestock died and the plague of hail in Exodus 9:13–26 (where livestock was again available for the plague of hail)).**

Then it hailed in Egypt like it never had before. The hail struck and killed everything in the fields. The only place it did not hail was in the land of Goshen, where the Israelites were. But as usual, Pharaoh called Moses and Aaron to pray the plague away and when it was gone, he and his officials hardened their hearts once more.

The Plague of Locusts
Then the Lord said to Moses, "Go to Pharaoh, for I have hardened his heart and the hearts of his officials so that I may perform these miraculous signs of mine amongst them that you may tell your children and grandchildren how I dealt harshly with the Egyptians and how I performed my signs amongst them, and that you may know that I am the Lord." So Moses and Aaron went to Pharaoh and told him all that the Lord had said and that if he did not let the people go, a plague of locusts would come over the land like nothing their mothers and fathers had ever seen before. So Pharaoh partially agreed. He agreed that the men only could go. Moses told Pharaoh that they must go with their young and old, their sons and daughters and with their flocks and herds since they were to celebrate a festival to the Lord. But Pharaoh told Moses that they were up to evil and he would only allow the men to go.

So the Lord commanded Moses to stretch forth his hand over Egypt and the Lord made an east wind blow across the land all that day and night. By morning the wind brought the locusts and they invaded Egypt in great numbers. They covered all the ground until it was black and they devoured everything that was left after the hail—everything growing in the fields and the fruit on the trees. Nothing green remained on any tree or plant in all of Egypt. Pharaoh repented before Moses and Aaron and asked for their God to take the deadly plague away. As usual Moses and Pharaoh left and prayed to God and God sent a west wind which caught hold of the locusts and carried them into the Red Sea. No locust could be found anywhere in Egypt, but the Lord hardened Pharaoh's heart, and he would not let the Israelites go.

The Plague of Darkness
The Lord said to Moses, "Stretch out your hand toward the sky so that darkness would spread over Egypt—darkness that can be felt." So Moses stretched out his hand toward the sky, and total darkness covered all Egypt for three days. No one could see anyone else or leave his place for three days. Yet all the Israelites had light in the places where they lived.

So Pharaoh pleaded with Moses and Aaron and Pharaoh told them that they could go, their women and children could go, but they must leave their flocks and herds behind. Moses told him that he must allow them to have sacrifices and burnt offerings to present to their God and so the livestock must go too. But the Lord hardened Pharaoh's heart and he was not willing to let them go. Then Pharaoh said to Moses, "Get out of my sight! Make sure that you do not appear before me again! The day you see my face you will die." "Just as you say," Moses replied, "I will never appear before you again."

The Plague on the Firstborn and the Passover
In the first month of the New Year, the Lord told Moses that He would bring a plague on Pharaoh and on Egypt and all the firstborn children would die. The Lord said, "After

116

this plague, he will let you go. He will drive you out completely."

The Lord also instructed Moses that the Israelites should choose a year-old lamb without defect and on the fourteenth day of the month, the lamb must be slaughtered at twilight. He gave them specific instructions as to how to eat and to discard of the unused meat. Very importantly, they were to take some of the blood and put it on the sides and tops of the door frames of the houses where they ate the lambs. On that same night, the Lord instructed that He would pass through Egypt and strike down every firstborn—both men and animals and would bring judgment on all the gods of Egypt. The blood was to be a sign for the Israelites on the houses where they were; and when He saw the blood, He would pass over those houses and no destructive plague would touch those houses when He struck Egypt.

Then the Lord told Moses that the day of the Passover was a day the Israelites were to commemorate for generations to come—it was to be celebrated as a festival to the Lord as a lasting ordinance. They were to eat bread made without yeast for seven days. They were also to celebrate the Feast of the Unleavened Bread as a lasting ordinance for generations to come because it was on that day that He brought the divisions out of Egypt. They were also instructed to hold a sacred assembly on the first day of the week and another one on the seventh day. On those two days, they were to do no work except to prepare food to eat. The Passover occurred in the month of Abib (**which would occur in the months of March/April in modern calendar times**).

Then Moses went and gathered all the elders of Egypt and gave them the instructions as God gave them to him. Then the people bowed down and worshipped and they did just what the Lord commanded Moses and Aaron. At about midnight, the Lord went through Egypt. Every firstborn child of the Egyptians died, from the firstborn of Pharaoh, who sat on the throne, to the firstborn of every slave girl, and all the firstborn of the cattle as well. There was a loud wailing throughout Egypt worse than there ever was before, for there was not a house of the Egyptians without someone dead in it. However, amongst the Israelites no firstborn died.

THE EXODUS

The Israelites Leave Egypt

After the plague of the firstborn hit Egypt, Pharaoh summoned Moses and Aaron during the night and told them to take their women, children, flocks and herds and leave. And Pharaoh told Moses that before he (Moses left), Moses should bless him! The Egyptians urged the Israelites to leave quickly as they feared that if the Israelites tarried, all the Egyptians would die.

As Moses had instructed, the Israelites asked the Egyptians for gold, silver and clothing. The Lord made the Egyptians favourably disposed to the Israelites and the Egyptians gave the Israelites whatever they asked for. The Israelites journeyed from Egypt to Succoth and there were six hundred thousand men on foot excluding women and children. They had lived in Egypt 430 years. At the end of 430 years, to the very day, all the Lord's divisions left Egypt. Because the Lord kept vigil that night to bring them out of Egypt, on that night, all the Israelites were instructed to keep vigil to honour the Lord for the generations to come.

The Lord also asked Moses to have every firstborn consecrated. The first offspring amongst the womb of the Israelites was to belong to the Lord, whether man or animal. The firstborn man was to be redeemed and set aside for service to the Lord and the animal was to be used as a sacrifice or burnt offering to the Lord. So Moses reminded the people to observe the requirements of the Lord to keep the Passover.

Crossing the Red Sea

God guided the Israelites through the desert road toward the Red Sea. He knew that if He guided them through the

119

land of the Philistines, though it was shorter, if they faced war, they would turn around and go back to Egypt. Moses remembered and took Joseph's bones with him. The Lord led them by day in a pillar of cloud and by night in a pillar of fire to give them light.

Then the Lord told Moses to have the people encamp near to the sea as He would harden Pharaoh's heart once more and Pharaoh would pursue them. God said, "I will gain glory for myself through Pharaoh and all his army, and the Egyptians will know that I am the Lord." So the Israelites encamped near to the sea. When Pharaoh was told that the people had fled, he changed his mind and pursued the Israelites. He took six hundred of the best chariots together with other chariots out of Egypt, with officers over all of them.

When the Israelites saw Pharaoh's army coming after them, they were terrified and cried out to their Lord. They said to Moses, "Was it because there were no graves in Egypt that you brought us out to the desert to die? What have you done to us by bringing us out of Egypt? Didn't we say to you in Egypt, 'Leave us alone; let us serve the Egyptians'? It would have been better for us to serve the Egyptians than to die in the desert." Moses answered the people, "Do not be afraid. Stand firm and you will see the deliverance the Lord will bring you today. The Egyptians you see today you will never see again. The Lord will fight for you; you only need to be still." Then God told Moses to raise his staff and stretch it out over the sea to divide the water so that the Israelites could go through the sea on dry land. Then the angel of God, who had been travelling in front of Israel's army, withdrew from in front of the Israelites and went behind them. The pillar of cloud also moved from in front of them and stood behind them, coming between the armies of Israel and the armies of Egypt. Throughout the night, the cloud brought darkness to the one side and light to the other side so that neither army went near the other all night long.

When Moses stretched out his hand over the sea, all that night, the Lord drove back the sea with a strong east wind and turned it into dry land. The waters were divided and the Israelites went through the sea on dry ground with a wall of water on their right and a wall of water on their left. The Egyptians pursued the Israelites and all Pharaoh's horses and chariots and horsemen followed them into the sea. During the last watch of the night the Lord looked down from the pillar of fire and cloud at the Egyptian army and threw it into confusion. He made the wheels from their chariots fall off so that they had difficulty driving. The Egyptians realised that God was fighting for the Israelites and said, "Let's get away from the Israelites! The Lord is fighting for them against Egypt."

God then instructed Moses to raise his staff over the sea so that the water may flow back into its place and over the Egyptians, their chariots and horsemen. Moses did so. At daybreak, the water went back into its place. The Egyptians were fleeing toward it and the Lord swept them up into the sea. None of the Egyptian army that followed the Israelites into the sea, survived. They all drowned. But the Israelites went through the sea on dry ground, with a wall of water on their right and a wall of water on their left. That day, the Lord saved Israel from the hand of the Egyptians, and Israel saw the Egyptians lying dead on the shore. When the Israelites saw the great power the Lord displayed against the Egyptians, the people feared the Lord and put their trust in Him and in His servant, Moses.

GOD PROVIDES FOR THE ISRAELITES IN THE DESERT

The Waters at Marah

When the Israelites were led out by Moses through the Red Sea, they travelled for three days without finding any water. They came to a place called Marah, but they could not drink the water because it was bitter (that is why the place is called Marah). So the Israelites murmured against Moses, as they had no water to drink. Moses cried out to the Lord who showed him a piece of wood. Moses threw the wood into the water and the water became sweet.

There the Lord made a decree and a law for the Israelites and tested them. He said, "If you listen carefully to the voice of the Lord, your God and do what is right in his eyes, if you pay attention to his commands and keep all his decrees, I will not bring you any of the diseases I brought on the Egyptians, for I am the Lord, who heals you." Then they came to a place called Elim, where there were twelve springs and seventy palm trees and they encamped there near the water.

Manna and Quail

The Israelites ran out of food after about two months in the desert (after they had left Egypt). They murmured against Moses again saying that it was best that they had been left to die in Egypt as there they had pots of food they could eat whenever they wanted but Moses instead had brought them out in the desert to starve to death. So the Lord said to Moses, "I will rain down bread from Heaven for you. The people are to go out each day and gather enough for that day and none was to be kept as left overs for the next day. In this way, I will test them and see whether they will follow my instructions. On the sixth day, they are to prepare what they bring in, and that is to be twice as much as they gathered on the other days."

So Moses went to the people and told them what God intended to do. He said to them, "Who are we that you should grumble against us. You are not grumbling against us, but against the Lord." He continued, "You will know that it was the Lord when he gives you meat in the evening and all the bread you want in the morning." That evening, quail came and covered the camp. The next morning, thin flakes like frost appeared on the desert floor. The Israelites did not know what it was, so Moses told them that it was the bread that the Lord had given them to eat and he gave them the instructions as God had given them to him. Some of the Israelites did not listen and they kept part of the bread until the next morning. By then, it was full of maggots and began to smell, so Moses became angry with them.

The Sabbath

The Lord commanded that the seventh day was to be a day of rest, a holy Sabbath to the Lord. So He told them to bake and boil what they needed to on the sixth day and to save what was left until the seventh day. So Moses told the people that on the sixth day they were to gather enough of the bread for the seventh day, the Sabbath, as there would not be anything to collect on the Sabbath. However, some of the people still went out on the seventh day to gather it, but they found none. The Lord said to Moses, "How long will you refuse to keep my commands and my instructions? Bear in mind that the Lord has given you the Sabbath and that is why on the sixth day he gives you bread for two days. Everyone is to stay where he is on the seventh day; no one is to go out." So the people rested on the seventh day.

The people of Israel called the bread manna. It was white like coriander seed and tasted like wafers made with honey. Moses said, "This is what the Lord has commanded: Take an omer, (a tenth of an ephah or (**3.7 litres**)) of manna and keep it for generations to come, so that they can see the bread I gave you to eat in the desert when I brought you out of Egypt." Moses and Aaron did as the Lord commanded. The Israelites ate manna for forty years until they came to a land that was settled at the border of Canaan.

Water from the Rock
The Israelites set out from a desert called the Desert of Sin, travelling from place to place as the Lord was commanding them. But they quarreled with Moses (as they had no water to drink). They said, "Give us water to drink." Moses asked them, "Why do you quarrel with me? Why do you put the Lord to the test?" But the people were thirsty for water there, and they grumbled against Moses. They said, "Why did you bring us up out of Egypt to make us and our children and livestock die of thirst?" Then Moses cried out to the Lord, "What am I to do with these people? They are almost ready to stone me." The Lord answered Moses, "Walk on ahead of the people. Take with you some of the elders of Israel and take in your hand the staff with which you struck the Nile and go. I will stand there before you by the rock at Horeb. Strike the rock, and water will come out of it for the people to drink." So Moses did this in the sight of the elders of Israel. And he called the place Massah and Meribah because the Israelites quarreled and because they tested the Lord saying, "Is the Lord among us or not?"

Moses is Visited by His Father-in-Law and is Reunited with His Family
Moses' father-in-law visited him after he heard of everything that God was doing for Moses and how the Lord had brought Israel out of Egypt. Moses had sent his wife,

Zipporah and their two sons back to Jethro whilst he was delivering the Israelites from Egypt. So Jethro, Zipporah and her two sons returned and came to meet Moses in the wilderness where he was camping near the mountain of God. After they greeted each other, Moses took Jethro to the tent and told him of everything the Lord had done to Pharaoh and the Egyptians for Israel's sake and about the hardships they had met along the way and how the Lord had saved them.

Jethro Praises God
Jethro was delighted to hear about all the good things the Lord had done for Israel in rescuing them from the hand of the Egyptians. He said, "Praise be to the Lord, who rescued you from the hand of the Egyptians and of Pharaoh, and who rescued the people from the hand of the Egyptians. Now I know that the Lord is greater than all other gods, for he did this to those who treated Israel arrogantly." Then Jethro brought a burnt offering and other sacrifices to God, and Aaron came with all the elders of Israel to eat a meal with Moses' father-in-law in the presence of God.

Jethro Advises Moses
The next day Moses took his seat to serve as judge for the people and they stood around him from morning until evening. When Jethro saw this, he told Moses that what he was doing was not good and that he would only wear himself out. He told Moses that the work was too heavy for him and that he could not handle it alone. Jethro then gave Moses some advice. He advised him that he should be the people's representative before God and that he should bring the disputes of the people before God. He was to teach them His decrees and instructions, show them the way they were to live and how they were to behave. However, he was then to select capable men from the

people—men who feared God, trustworthy men who hated dishonest gain, and appoint them as officials over thousands, hundreds, fifties and tens. He should have them serve as judges for the people at all times but have them bring every difficult case to him. The simple cases they could decide themselves. He encouraged Moses that the suggested approach would make his load lighter because the other men would share the load with him. Jethro then told Moses that if he did this, and if God so commanded, he would be able to stand the strain, and all the people would go home satisfied.

Moses Listens to His Father-In-Law's Advice
Moses listened to his father-in-law and did everything he said. He chose capable men from all Israel and made them leaders of the people, officials over thousands, hundreds, fifties and tens. They served as judges for the people at all times. The difficult cases they brought to Moses, but the simple ones they decided themselves. Then Moses sent his father-in-law on his way and Jethro returned to his own country.

THE ISRAELITES AT WAR WITH THE AMALEKITES

The Amalekites came and attacked the Israelites whilst they were camped at a place called Rephidim. Moses said to Joshua, "Choose some of our men and go out to fight the Amalekites. Tomorrow, I will stand on top of the hill with the staff of God in my hands." So Joshua fought the Amalekites as Moses had ordered and Moses, Aaron and Hur (one of the elders) went to the top of the hill. As long as Moses held up his hands, the Israelites were winning, but whenever he lowered his hands, the Amalekites were winning. When Moses' hands grew tired, they took a stone and put it under him and he sat on it. Aaron and Hur held his hands up—one on one side, one on the other—so that his hands remained steady until sunset. So Joshua overcame the Amalekite army with the sword.

Then the Lord said to Moses, "Write this on a scroll as something to be remembered and make sure that Joshua hears it, because I will blot out the memory of Amalek from under Heaven." Moses built an altar and called it 'The Lord is my Banner'. He said, "For hands were lifted up to the throne of the Lord. The Lord will be at war against the Amalekites from generation to generation."

THE TEN COMMANDMENTS AND OTHER LAWS GIVEN TO THE ISRAELITES

God Descends on Mount Sinai

In the third month after the Israelites left Egypt, God appeared to Moses and told him that if the Israelites kept His covenant, then out of all nations, they would be His treasured nation. The Israelites confirmed to Moses that they would do everything that the Lord had said. The Lord also told Moses that He was going to come to him in a dense cloud, so that the people could hear Him speaking with him and as a result of this, they would always put their trust in Moses.

God instructed Moses to consecrate the people and have them wash their clothes, abstain from sexual relations and be ready for the third day because on that day the Lord would come down to Mount Sinai in the sight of the people. He told him to ensure that no person or animal went up to the mountain or touched the foot of it, as whoever did so would surely be put to death (but they were to be put to death by stone or by arrows—not a hand was to be laid on those persons or animals). So Moses did as the Lord commanded.

On the morning of the third day of the third month, thunder and lightning accompanied a thick cloud which appeared over the mountain together with a very loud trumpet blast. Mount Sinai was covered with smoke as the Lord descended on it in fire. The entire mountain trembled violently and the trumpet grew louder and louder. Then Moses spoke and the voice of God answered him.

The Lord descended to the top of Mount Sinai and called Moses to the top of the mountain; so Moses went up. God told Moses to go down and warn the people not to force their way through to see the Lord as many of them would perish if they did so. But Moses assured the Lord that, as He had instructed and warned, limits were placed around the mountain and it was set apart as holy. Therefore, the people could not come up to Mount Sinai. So the Lord told him to go down and bring up Aaron but the priests and the people must not force their way through. Moses went down to the people and spoke to them as the Lord had spoken to him.

The Ten Commandments
And God spoke these words:

1. "I am the Lord your God, who brought you out of Egypt, out of the land of slavery. You shall have no other gods before me.
2. You shall not make for yourself an idol in the form of anything in heaven above or on the earth beneath or in the waters below. You shall not bow down to them nor worship them; for I, the Lord your God, am a jealous God, punishing the children for the sin of the fathers down to the third and fourth generation of those who hate me, but showing love to a thousand generations of those who love me and keep my commandments.
3. You shall not misuse the name of the Lord, your God, for the Lord will not hold anyone guiltless who misuses his name.
4. Remember the Sabbath day by keeping it holy. Six days you shall labour and do all your work, but the seventh day is a Sabbath to the Lord your God. On it you will not do any work, neither you, nor your son nor daughter, nor your manservant nor maidservant, nor your animals, nor the aliens within your gates. For in six days the Lord made the heavens and the earth, the sea, and all that is in

129

them, but he rested on the seventh day. Therefore, the Lord blessed the Sabbath day and made it holy.

5. Honour your father and your mother, so that you may live long in the land that the Lord your God is giving you.
6. You shall not murder.
7. You shall not commit adultery.
8. You shall not steal.
9. You shall not bear false testimony against your neighbor.
10. You shall not covet your neighbour's house. You shall not covet your neighbour's wife, or his male servant or his female servant, his ox or donkey, or anything that belongs to your neighbor."

Idols and Altars
The Lord specifically told Moses to warn the Israelites against making other gods and altars. He said, "You have seen for yourselves that I have spoken to you from heaven: Do not make any gods to be alongside me; do not make for yourselves gods of silver or gods of gold."

Other Laws
The Lord also gave other laws as to how to deal with Hebrew servants, personal injuries, protection of property, justice, mercy and the Sabbath in chapters 21–23 of Exodus.

The Three Annual Festivals
The Lord also commanded the Israelites to celebrate three different festivals to Him at three different times of the year, namely (i) the Feast of the Unleavened Bread. In the month of Abib, the month they came out of Egypt. For seven days they were to eat bread made without yeast; (ii) the Feast of the Harvest with the first fruits of the crops they sowed in their fields; and (iii) the Feast of In-

Gathering. This should happen at the end of the year when they gathered in their crops from the field.

Moses Receives Instructions to Build the Tabernacle
The Lord called Moses, Aaron, Nadab and Abihu and seventy of the elders up to Him. He told all except Moses that they were to worship from afar as only Moses alone was to approach Him. When Moses was close to Him, He confirmed the covenant with Moses and gave Moses instructions on the building of a tabernacle so that He could dwell amongst the Israelites. **A tabernacle is a place or house of worship. The building of this tabernacle signifies the building of the first church. It would become a portable sanctuary through which the Israelites would carry the ark of the Lord's covenant through the desert.**

He gave instructions on what the Israelites were to bring as an offering for the tabernacle - articles including gold, silver, bronze, blue, purple and scarlet yarn and fine linen. The tabernacle was to have an ark (the Ark of the Covenant) and He gave him specific instructions as to how to build it. He told him that it would be over the ark that He would meet with him and give him all His commands for the Israelites. The tabernacle was to have a table made with specific details on which the bread of the Presence (manna) was to be placed, and which was to be before Him at all times.

A lampstand was also to be placed in the tabernacle, an altar of burnt offering was to be built for the tabernacle and the tabernacle was also to have a courtyard. He gave specific instructions as to how the lampstand, the tabernacle and the courtyard were to be constructed. These specific instructions can be found in chapters 25–27 of Exodus. He gave other instructions as to the consecration of the priests, the altar of incense, atonement money, basin for washing, anointing oil and incense. These specific instructions can be found in chapters 28–31 of Exodus.

The Sabbath
Then He said to Moses, "Say to the Israelites, 'You must observe the Sabbaths. This will be a sign between me and you for the generations to come, so you may know that I am the Lord, who makes you holy.'" When the Lord had finished speaking to Moses on Mount Sinai, He gave him the two tablets of the Testimony (the tablets of stone which God inscribed by the finger of God).

THE GOLDEN CALF

Moses stayed on the mountain whilst God spoke to him for a while. When the people saw that Moses took long to come down from the mountain, they gathered around Aaron and told him that since they did not know what had happened to Moses, the one who brought them out of Egypt, they should make gods who would go before them. So Aaron told them to remove their jewels and bring them to him. He took what they brought and with a tool, made the jewelry into an idol, cast in the shape of a calf. Then they said, "These are your gods, O Israel, who brought you up out of Egypt."

When Aaron saw it, he built an altar in front of the calf and announced, "Tomorrow there will be a festival to the Lord." So the next day, the people arose early and sacrificed burnt offerings and presented fellowship offerings. And they ate, drank and were merry with noise. Then the Lord told Moses to go down to the people because they had become corrupt and had been quick to turn away from what they were commanded. He told Moses that they had made themselves a golden calf and bowed down to it and sacrificed to it saying that, "These are your gods, O Israel, who brought you up out of Egypt. 'I have seen these people and they are a stiff-necked (**haughtily stubborn**) people. Now leave me alone so that my anger may burn against them and that I may destroy them. Then I will make you into a great nation.'"

But Moses sought the favour of the Lord, his God. He asked God not to destroy them as He was the one to bring them out of Egypt; lest the Egyptians say that the Lord had brought them out of Egypt to kill them in the mountains and wipe them off the face of the earth. He pleaded with the Lord to turn from His anger and for Him to remember

Abraham, Isaac and Jacob and the covenant He had made with them. Then the Lord relented and did not bring on His people, the disaster He had threatened.

Moses left God's presence and went down the mountain with the two tablets of the Testimony in his hands. They were inscribed on both sides, front and back. They were the work of God and the writing engraved on the tablets was the writing of God. When Moses approached the camp and saw the calf and the dancing, he was angry and he threw the tablets out of his hands, breaking them into pieces at the foot of the mountain. He took the calf and burned it in the fire, then he ground it to powder, scattered it on the water and made the Israelites drink it. He then quarreled with Aaron and asked him, "What did these people do to you that you led them into such great sin." Aaron responded, "Do not be angry my lord. You know how prone these people are to evil and they said to me that I should make them gods who will go before us because they did not know what happened to this fellow Moses who brought us out of Egypt."

Moses told the people that they had committed a great sin, but that he would go up to the Lord to see if he could make atonement for their sin. So Moses went back up to the Lord. Moses asked God to forgive the sin of the people and if He would not, then blot him (Moses) out of the book that He had written. But God said to Moses, "Whoever has sinned against me, I will blot out of my book. When the time is right, I will punish them for their sin." And the Lord struck the people with a plague because of what they did with the calf Aaron made.

MOSES AND THE GLORY OF THE LORD

God is Angry with the Israelites
The Lord then told Moses to lead the Israelites to the place He had spoken to Moses about and that an angel of the Lord would go before them. He told him that He would not go with them because the people were stubborn and if He went, He might destroy them. He commanded the Israelites to take off their ornaments and that He, the Lord, would decide what to do with them. So they stripped off their ornaments at Mount Horeb.

Moses told the Lord that if His presence was not going with them then He should not send them from where they were. He said to the Lord, "How will anyone know that you are pleased with me and with your people unless you go with us? What else will distinguish me and your people from all the other people on the face of the earth?" And the Lord said to Moses, "I will do the very thing you have asked, because I am pleased with you and I know you by name." Then Moses said to the Lord, "Now show me your glory." The Lord told him that He would cause all His goodness to pass in front of him and that He would proclaim His name, the Lord in his presence. He said, "I will have mercy on whom I will have mercy, and I will have compassion on whom I will have compassion, but you cannot see my face, for no one may see me and live." Then the Lord said to him, "There is a place near me where you may stand on a rock. When my glory passes by, I will put you in a cleft of the rock and cover you with my hand until I have passed by. Then I will remove my hand and you will see my back; but my face must not be seen."

The New Stone Tablets
God told Moses to chisel out two stone tablets like the first ones and that he would write on them the words that were

on the first tablets which he had broken. God told him that he was to go to Mount Sinai the following day by himself. No one was to go with him and no one was to be seen anywhere near the mountain, including animals. So Moses did as God instructed.

Then the Lord came down in the cloud and stood there with him and proclaimed His name, the Lord. And He passed in front of Moses, proclaiming: "The Lord, the Lord, the compassionate and gracious God, slow to anger, abounding in love and faithfulness, maintaining love to the thousands, and forgiving wickedness, rebellion and sin. Yet he does not leave the guilty unpunished; he punishes the children and their children for the sin of the fathers to the third and fourth generation." Moses bowed down to the ground and worshipped and he prayed and pleaded with the Lord to go with the Israelites although they were stiff-necked. He asked the Lord to forgive their wickedness and their sin and take them as His inheritance. So the Lord made a covenant with Moses as He had done with Abraham, Isaac and Jacob, and with the same terms. Moses was on Mount Sinai for forty days and forty nights without eating bread or drinking water. And he wrote on the tablets the words of the covenant—The Ten Commandments.

The Radiant Face of Moses
When Moses came down from Mount Sinai with the two tablets of the Testimony in his hands, he was not aware that as a result of him speaking to the Lord, his face had grown radiant. When the Israelites saw the radiance on his face, they were afraid to go near him but Moses made them comfortable and so they went and spoke to him and he gave them all the commands of the Lord. When Moses finished speaking to them, he put a veil over his face, but whenever he entered the Lord's presence to speak with Him, he removed the veil until he came out of God's presence and

the Israelites would see his radiance. Then Moses put the veil back over his face until he went back in to speak to the Lord.

The Commands of the Lord
So Moses told the people about the Sabbath regulations, the building of the tabernacle, the ark, the altars, the materials to be used in the building of the tabernacle, every measurement and detail, and how to make the priestly garments. Then when they had built the tabernacle and set it up on the first day of the first month, as the Lord had instructed, the cloud covered the Tent of Meeting (a tent Moses regularly pitched outside the camp, some distance away so that anyone enquiring of the Lord would go into the tent outside the camp), and the glory of the Lord filled the tabernacle. Moses could not enter the Tent of Meeting because the cloud had settled upon it, and the glory of the Lord had filled the tabernacle.

In all the travels of the Israelites, whenever the cloud lifted from above the tabernacle, they would set out; but if the cloud did not lift, they did not set out—until the day it lifted. So the cloud of the Lord was over the tabernacle by day and the fire was in the cloud by night, in the sight of all the house of Israel during all their travels.

STORIES OF LEVITICUS

Leviticus is the title given to the third book of the Bible. It is the third book accredited to Moses and the third book of the Pentateuch. The name Leviticus derives from the word "Levi" pertaining to the Levite, the tribe of Levi whom the priests and others consecrated specifically to worship and who were specifically chosen by God. The book is very legalistic in nature and primarily shows the difference between the holiness of God and man's sinfulness. In order to have a full appreciation of the religious activities that are expected of the Israelites in the book which follows it— Numbers, an appreciation for Leviticus is necessary. It deals specifically with laws including those concerning sacrifice, the conduct of the people one to another and the holiness of the priests. It discusses the holy ceremonies which the Israelites were expected to celebrate for generations to come, the Day of Atonement and reiterates the importance of the Sabbath. Emphasis is also placed on obedience to the laws which God specified must be obeyed, together with the connected promises if they were obeyed and the consequential punishment, if they were not obeyed. Many of the principles and the various offerings are not practised by Christians today, as the coming of Christ represented the ultimate sacrifice and payment for sin of those who believe that He is the Christ. However, the command relating to the tithe (which was not attached to sin) and which is illustrated clearly in Leviticus, is still a relevant command today and one which Christians are encouraged to obey.

OFFERINGS

Burnt Offerings

God also spoke to Moses about various types of offerings which the Israelites should offer to God and the specific instructions when offering the various types of offerings. These offerings included:

- Burnt offerings (to be made with animals)
- Grain offerings (to be made with grain)
- Fellowship offerings (to be made with animals)
- Sin offerings (to be made with bulls and goats)
- Guilt offerings (to be made with ram from flock)

Clean and Unclean Food

Of land creatures, the Israelites were to eat only animals that both chewed their cud and had split hooves. Of sea creatures, they were to eat only creatures that had fins and scales. He also forbade the Israelites from eating blood.

Incest

The Lord gave the Israelites specific instructions against incest and clearly told them the persons with whom they could have sexual relations.

Prohibition Against Consulting Mediums and Spiritists

God also warned the Israelites against consulting mediums and spiritists and from prostituting themselves by following such mediums and spiritists.

FEASTS APPOINTED FOR THE ISRAELITES

The following are the appointed feasts which the Lord gave Moses to proclaim to the Israelites as sacred assemblies. **They are still applicable today**:

The Sabbath
They were told that there were six days when work could be done, but the seventh day was to be a Sabbath of rest, a day of sacred assembly. On that day, no work was to be done wherever the Israelites lived. It was to be a Sabbath to the Lord. **Today, the Sabbath is still generally celebrated as a day of rest or time of worship. In most religions and countries, it is a time made holy to God and is either observed on Saturday or Sunday.**

The Passover and Unleavened Bread
The Lord's Passover was to begin at twilight on the 14th day of the first month. On the 15th day of that month the Lord's Feast of Unleavened Bread was to begin: for seven days no bread made with yeast was to be eaten.

First fruits
When crops were planted in Canaan, the Israelites were to bring an offering of the first fruit of the grain that was harvested.

Feast of Weeks
From the day after the Sabbath, the day after the first fruit offering was brought, the Israelites were instructed to count off fifty days up to the day after the seventh Sabbath and then present an offering of new grain to the Lord. God also told the Israelites that when they reaped the harvest, they were not to reap the very edges of their field or gather the gleanings of their harvest. They were to leave them for the poor and the aliens.

Feasts of Trumpets

On the first day of the seventh month, there was to be a day of rest, a sacred assembly commemorated with trumpet blasts. On this day, no regular work was to be done and an offering made to the Lord by fire was to be presented.

Day of Atonement

The tenth day of the seventh month was to be the Day of Atonement. On that day, a sacred assembly was to be held and the Israelites were to deny themselves and present an offering made to the Lord by fire. No work was to be done on that day as it was to be the Day of Atonement, when atonement was made for the sin of the Israelites before the Lord.

Feast of Tabernacles

On the 15th day of the seventh month the Lord's Feast of the Tabernacles was to begin and it was to last for seven days. The first day was to be a sacred day and no regular work was to be done. For seven days, offerings to the Lord by fire were to be presented. On the eighth day, a sacred assembly was to be held and offerings, made to the Lord by fire were to be presented. The eighth day was appointed for the closing of the assembly and no regular work was to be done on that day.

THE TITHE

The Lord commanded Moses that a tithe (a tenth) of everything from the land, whether grain from the soil or fruit from the trees, belonged to the Lord. It is holy to the Lord. God told Moses that if a man redeemed any of his tithes, he must add a fifth to the value of it. The entire tithe of the herd and flock—every tenth animal that passed under the shepherd's rod would be holy to the Lord. The Lord said that men must not pick out the good from the bad or make any substitution. If he did make a substitution, both the animal and its substitute were to be deemed holy and could not be redeemed.

STORIES OF NUMBERS

Numbers is the fourth book of the Bible written by Moses (and perhaps later scribes and editors from later periods in Israel's history) and also forms part of the Pentateuch. Numbers is made up of law and history and communicates the story of Israel's journey from Mount Sinai to the Plains of Moab on the border of Canaan—the Promised Land. It reveals the battle that the Israelites had to remain holy and trusting in God and showed God's judgment on them as a result of not being able to remain holy and trusting. The book begins with God commanding Moses to take a census of the Israelites and to organize them into military camps. Here God begins to set up the Israelites to overtake in battle on their way to the Promised Land. It demonstrates in many areas, the Israelites' continuous complaints against God and Moses in spite of God's grace and mercy toward them and reveals God's wrath toward them in response. At the same time, it also demonstrates God's renewed grace and His willingness to forgive is also evident. Even Miriam, Aaron and Moses were not exempt from God's wrath and each would suffer his or her own consequence as a result of disobedience to God. It offers the experiences of the first and second generation of the Israelites whilst they were led to wander in the wilderness for forty years (as a consequence of disobedience) before arriving to the Promised Land. It ends with the Israelites being on the Plains of Moab in anticipation of entering the Promised Land. The stories and principles are equally applicable in modern times as they illustrate how God pronounces His blessing, follows through on His blessing but at the same time, punishes disobedience to His word.

FIRST CENSUS

The Lord spoke to Moses in the Tent of Meeting in the Desert of Sinai on the first day of the second month of the second year after the Israelites came out of Egypt. He told Moses to take a census of the entire Israelite community by their clans and families, listing every man by name, one by one. He told him and Aaron that they were to number by their divisions, all the men in Israel twenty years and older who were able to serve in the army. Moses and Aaron were to take one man from each tribe, each the head of his family to help him and He gave them the names of the men who were to help them.

Of the tribe of Levi, the Lord told Moses that he was not to count them amongst the others. They were not to be included in the census. Instead, the Levites were to be appointed to be in charge of the tabernacle of the Testimony—over all its furnishings and everything belonging to it. They were to carry the tabernacle and all its furnishings and they were to take care of it and encamp around it. Whenever the tabernacle was to be set up or taken down, the Levites were to do it and anyone else who did it, not being a Levite, would be put to death. The Levites were to set up their tents around the tabernacle of the Testimony so that wrath would not fall on the Israelite community.

The Arrangement of the Tribal Camps

The Lord said to Moses and Aaron: "The Israelites are to camp around the Tent of Meeting some distance from it, each man under his standard with the banners of his family."

The divisions of the camp of Judah were to encamp under their standard on the east side toward the sunrise; the people of Judah (74,600 men) were to lead. The tribe of

Issachar (54,400 men) was to camp next to them; followed by the Tribe of Zebulun (57,400 men). All the men assigned to the Judah camp were 186,400.

On the south side were to be the divisions of the camp of Reuben under their standard. The people of Reuben (46,500 men) were to lead; the tribe of Simeon (59,300 men) was to camp next to them; then the tribe of Gad (45,650 men). All the men assigned to the Reuben camp were 151,450.

On the west side would be the divisions of the camp of Ephraim under their standard. The people of Ephraim (40,500 men) were to lead; the tribe of Manasseh (32,200 men) was to camp next to them; followed by the tribe of Benjamin (35,400 men). All the men assigned to the Ephraim camp were 108,100.

On the north side would be the divisions of the camp of Dan under their standard. The people of Dan (62,700 men) were to lead; the tribe of Asher (41,500 men) was to camp next to them; followed by the tribe of Naphtali (53,400 men). All the men assigned to the Dan camp were 157,600.

These were the Israelites counted according to their families. The total number was 603,550. So Moses and Aaron did as the Lord commanded and that is the way they encamped under their standards. The Levites set up themselves in the middle of the camp together with the Tent of Meeting. They were not counted along with the Israelites, as this was what the Lord had commanded Moses.

GOD HEARS THE ISRAELITES' COMPLAINTS

Fire from the Lord
The Israelites complained to Moses about their hardships and the Lord heard them. When the Lord heard them, His anger was aroused and He sent fire which burned amongst them and consumed some of the outskirts of the camp. The people then cried out to Moses and when Moses prayed, the fire died down. So the place was called Taberah, because the fire from the Lord had burned amongst them.

The Israelites then started to complain that they wanted meat to eat. They said that they remembered the fish they ate in Egypt at no cost, and the cucumbers, melons, leeks, onions and garlic, and said, "But now we have lost our appetite because now we never see anything but this manna." The manna was like coriander seed and looked like resin. It fell from Heaven every night when the dew settled on the camp at night. It tasted like something that was made with olive oil. When they gathered it, they ground it in a hand mill or crushed it in a mortar. They would cook it in a pot or make it into cakes.

Moses' Complaints to the Lord
Moses heard the people of every family wailing at the entrance of his tent and the Lord became exceedingly angry, which troubled Moses. So Moses went to the Lord, asking, "Why have you brought this trouble on your servant? What have I done to displease you that you put the burden of all these people on me? Did I conceive all these people? Did I give birth to them? Why do you tell me to carry them in my arms, as a nurse carries an infant, to the land you promised on oath to their forefathers? Where can I get meat for these people? They keep wailing to me, 'Give us meat to eat!' I cannot carry all these people by myself; the burden is too heavy for me. If this is how you

are going to treat me, put me to death right now, if I have found favour in your eyes, and do not let me face my own ruin."

God Divides the Burden of Moses
The Lord said to Moses: "Bring me seventy of Israel's elders who are known to you as leaders and officials amongst the people. Have them come to the Tent of Meeting that they may stand there with you. I will come down and speak with you there, and I will take the Spirit that is on you and put the Spirit on them. They will help you carry the burden of the people so that you will not have to carry it alone." Moses did as God told him and when the elders were gathered at the appointed place, the Lord came down in the cloud and spoke with Moses. The Lord took of the Spirit that was on Moses and put that Spirit on the seventy elders. When the Spirit was rested on them, they prophesied. When Moses was questioned about two of the elders prophesying in the camp, he said, "I wish that all the Lord's people were prophets and that the Lord would put his Spirit on them!"

The Lord Prepares the People for Meat
The Lord then instructed Moses as follows: "Tell the people: consecrate yourselves in preparation for tomorrow, when you will eat meat. The Lord heard you when you wailed, 'If only we had meat to eat! We were better off in Egypt!' Now the Lord will give you meat to eat, and you will eat it. You will not eat it just for one day, or two days, or five, ten or twenty days but for a whole month, until it comes out of your nostrils and you loathe it because you have rejected the Lord, who is amongst you, and have wailed before him, saying, 'Why did we ever leave Egypt.'" But Moses questioned whether he should indeed tell the people that God would provide meat for them for an entire month." God responded, "Is the Lord's arm too

147

short? You will see whether or not what I say will come true for you."

Quail from the Lord

A wind went out from the Lord and drove quail in from the sea. It brought them down all around the camp to about three feet above the ground, and as far as a day's walk in any direction. All that day and night and the next day, the people went out and gathered quail. They gathered in abundance and they spread them out all around the camp. But whilst the meat was still between their teeth and before it could be consumed, the anger of the Lord burned against the people and He struck them with a severe plague which caused many of them to die. They buried many of the people who had craved other food there and as a result, called the place Kibroth Hattaavah.

SIBLING RIVALRY

Miriam and Aaron Oppose Moses
Moses married a Cushite woman whom Miriam and Aaron did not favour. So they both began to speak against Moses saying, "Has the Lord spoken only through Moses? Hasn't he also spoken through us?" And the Lord heard it. Moses was a very humble man, more humble than anyone else on the face of the earth. So the Lord summoned Moses, Aaron and Miriam to come to the Tent of Meeting so that He could speak to them. He summoned Aaron and Miriam specifically when he came down in the pillar of cloud and both of them stepped forward.

God Scolds Aaron and Miriam
When they stepped forward, the Lord said, "Listen to my words:
When a prophet of the Lord is among you,
I reveal myself to him in visions; I speak to him in dreams,
But this is not true of my servant Moses; he is faithful in all my house.
With him I speak face to face, clearly and not in riddles;
He sees the form of the Lord.
Why then are you not afraid to speak against my servant Moses?"

Miriam is Punished with Leprosy
The anger of the Lord burned against Miriam and Aaron and He left them. When the cloud lifted from above the Tent, Miriam was leprous and stood as white as snow. Aaron realised that Miriam had leprosy and he said to Moses, "Please, my lord, do not hold against us the sin we have so foolishly committed. Do not let her be like a stillborn infant coming from her mother's womb with its flesh half eaten away."

So Moses cried out to the Lord to heal Miriam, but the Lord replied, "If her father had spit in her face, would she not have been in disgrace for seven days? Confine her outside the camp for seven days; after that she can be brought back." So Miriam was confined outside the camp for seven days, and the people did not move on to the next camping point at the Desert of Paran until she was brought back amongst them.

EXPLORING THE PROMISED LAND

Exploring the Promised Land
God commanded Moses to send some men to explore the land of Canaan, the land which He had planned to give to the Israelites. He commanded him to send one of the leaders of each ancestral tribe and gave him the names of the leaders of each ancestral tribe whom he was to send. The names of the men that went on the exploration were: Shammua, Shaphat, Caleb; Igal, Hoshea (whom Moses renamed Joshua), Palti, Gaddiel, Gaddi, Ammieel, Sethur, Nahbi and Guel.

Moses told the leaders of each tribe that they were to go up through the Negev and on to the hill country. They were to observe of the land, see what the land was like and whether its inhabitants were weak or strong, few or many. The leaders were to find out what kind of land Canaan was, whether it was good or bad; what the towns were like, whether they were un-walled or fortified. They were to check the soil to see whether it was fertile or poor. They were to check to see if there were trees and they were to bring back some of the fruit of the land. So the men did as Moses instructed and went up and explored the land. When they reached a certain valley, they cut off a branch bearing a single cluster of grapes and two of them carried it on a pole between them, along with some pomegranates and figs. The place was called the Valley of Eschol because of the cluster of grapes the Israelites cut off there. At the end of forty days they returned from exploring the land.

Report on the Exploration of the Promised Land
The leaders came back to Moses and Aaron and the entire Israelite community. They reported to the whole assembly and showed them the fruit of the land. They accounted to Moses, "We went into the land to which you sent us, and it

does flow with milk and honey! Here is its fruit. But the people who live there are powerful and the cities are fortified and very large. We even saw descendants of Anak, the Anakites there." **The Anakites were said by biblical scholars to be a race of people who resembled giants and who descended from the ancient Nephilim (children who were procreated from the Sons of God (fallen angels) and daughters of men)).** He continued, "The Amalekites live in the Negev; the Hittities, Jebusites and Amorites live in the hill country; and the Canaanites live near the sea along the Jordan."

One of the leaders, whose name was Caleb, silenced the people before Moses and said, "We should go up and take possession of the land, for we certainly can do it." But the men who had gone with him insisted that the Israelites could not attack the inhabitants of the land for they were stronger than they were. They reaffirmed that all the people in the land were of great size and they said, "We seemed like grasshoppers in our own eyes." He went on to say that the Israelites looked like grasshoppers in the sight of the inhabitants of Canaan also.

The Israelites Rebel Once Again
The Israelites started again to grumble against Moses and Aaron and the whole assembly said to them, "If only we had died in Egypt! Or in this desert! Why is the Lord bringing us to this land only to let us fall by the sword? Our wives and children will be taken as plunder. Wouldn't it be better for us to go back to Egypt?" And they said to each other, "We should chose a leader and go back to Egypt."

Then Moses and Aaron fell face down in front of the whole Israelite community gathered there. Joshua and Caleb reiterated to the people that the land that they had passed

152

through and explored was exceedingly good and that if the Lord continued to be pleased with the Israelites, He would lead them into that land, a land that was flowing with milk and honey, and that He would give it to them. They told the assemblies, "Only do not rebel against the Lord. And do not be afraid of the people of the land, because we will swallow them up. Their protection is gone, but the Lord is with us. Do not be afraid of them." But the whole assembly talked about stoning Joshua and Caleb.

Then the glory of the Lord appeared at the Tent of Meeting to all the Israelites. The Lord said to Moses, "How long will these people treat me with contempt? How long will they refuse to believe in me, in spite of all the miraculous signs I have performed amongst them? I will strike them down with a plague and destroy them, but I will make you into a nation greater and stronger than they." But Moses pleaded with God and told Him that the Egyptians would hear about it and that they would say that their God was not able to bring them into the land He promised them on oath, so He slaughtered them in the desert.

Then Moses said, "Now let the Lord's strength be displayed, just as you have declared: 'The Lord is slow to anger, abounding in love and forgiving sin and rebellion. Yet he does not leave the guilty unpunished; He punishes the children for the sin of the fathers to the third and fourth generation.' In accordance with your great love, forgive the sin of these people, just as you have pardoned them from the time they left Egypt until now." The Lord replied, "I have forgiven them, as you asked. Nevertheless, as surely as I live and as surely as the glory of the Lord fills the whole earth, not one of the men who saw my glory and the miraculous signs I performed in Egypt and in the desert but who disobeyed me and tested me ten times, not one of them will ever see the land I promised on oath to their

153

forefathers. No one who has treated me with contempt will ever see it. Because my servant Caleb has a different spirit and follows me wholeheartedly, I will bring him into the land he went to, and his descendants will inherit it. Since the Amalekites and Canaanites are living in the valleys, turn back tomorrow and set out toward the desert along the route to the Red Sea."

The Lord then said to Moses and Aaron: "How long will this wicked community grumble against me? I have heard the complaints of these grumbling Israelites. So tell them, 'As surely as I live, declares the Lord, I will do to you the very things I heard you say: In this desert your bodies will fall—every one of you twenty years old or more who was counted in the census and who has grumbled against me. Not one of you will enter the land I swore with uplifted hand to make your home, except Caleb son of Jephunneh and Joshua son of Nun. As for your children that you said would be taken as plunder, I will bring them to the land that you have rejected—but you—your bodies will fall in this desert. Your children will be shepherds here for forty years, suffering for your unfaithfulness, until the last of your bodies lies in the desert.

For forty years—one year for each of the days you explored the land—you will suffer for your sins and know what it is like to have me against you.' I, the Lord have spoken, and I will surely do these things to this whole wicked community, which has banded together against me. They will meet their end in this desert; here they will die." And it was so. Of the twelve that went to explore the land, God struck down every one of them except Caleb and Joshua. When Moses reported it to all the Israelites, they mourned bitterly. Early the next morning, they went toward the high hill country saying that they had sinned and they would go up and possess the land God had promised. Moses warned them against their actions as the Lord was not with them and that they were disobeying God's command. But they did not listen to Moses. They went up any way and were attacked and beaten down by the Amalekites and Canaanites that lived there.

INSURRECTION AMONGST THE ISRAELITES

In addition to choosing Moses as the leader of the Israelites, God chose and consecrated his brother Aaron and his descendants to be the priests for the Israelites. One day, Korah, a Levite descendant, together with some descendants of the Reubenites (Abiram, Dathan and On), became insolent and rose up against Moses. With them were 250 Israelites who were well known community leaders and who had been appointed members of the council. They came as a group to Moses and Aaron and told them that they had gone too far by trying to set themselves above the Lord's assembly. One of the insurrectionists told Moses and Aaron that the entire assembly was holy, every one of them and the Lord was also with the entire assembly (**and not only with them**).

Moses told him that in the morning, the Lord would chose who belonged to Him and who was holy and Moses warned them that the Levites had gone too far. Moses said, "Isn't it enough for you that the God of Israel has separated you from the rest of the Israelite community and brought you near himself to do the work at the Lord's tabernacle and to stand before the community and minister to them? He has brought you and all your fellow Levites near himself, but now you are trying to get the priesthood too (for Aaron's descendants were consecrated as the priesthood for the Israelites and God had commanded Moses and Aaron that only descendants of Aaron should come to burn incense before the Lord). It is against the Lord that you and all your followers have banded together. Who is Aaron that you should grumble against him?"

Then Moses summoned two of the insurrectionists but they sent a message saying, "We will not come! Isn't it enough that you brought us up out of a land flowing with milk and honey to kill us in the desert? And now you also want to lord it over us? Moreover, you haven't brought us into a land flowing with milk and honey or given us an inheritance of fields and vineyards. Will you gouge out the eyes of these men? No, we will not come!" Then Moses became very angry and said to the Lord, "Do not accept their offering. I have not taken so much as a donkey from them, nor have I wronged any of them." The next day, when they all presented themselves to the Lord, the glory of the Lord appeared to the entire assembly. The Lord said to Moses and Aaron, "Separate yourselves from this assembly so that I can put an end to them at once." But Moses and Aaron fell face down and cried out, "O God, God of the spirits of all mankind, will you be angry with the entire assembly when only one man sins?" So the Lord told Moses to tell the assembly to move away from the tents of the Levites that had risen up against Moses and Aaron.

Then Moses told the assembly, "This is how you will know that the Lord has sent me to do all these things and that it was not my idea: If these men die a natural death and experience only what usually happens to men, then the Lord has not sent me. But if the Lord brought about something totally new, and the earth opens its mouth and swallows them, with everything that belongs to them, and they go down alive in the grave, then you will know that these men have treated the Lord with contempt."

As soon as Moses had finished speaking, the ground under them split apart and opened up its mouth and swallowed them up, with their households and all their possessions. They went down alive into the grave, with everything they owned; the earth closed over them, and they perished and were gone from the community. At their cries, all the Israelites amongst them fled, shouting, "The earth is going to swallow us too!" Fire then came out from the Lord and consumed the 250 men that followed the Reubenites and the Levites.

The next day, the whole Israelite community grumbled against Moses and Aaron. "You have killed the Lord's people," they said, and they gathered in opposition to Moses and Aaron and turned toward the Tent of Meeting. Suddenly the cloud covered the Tent and the glory of the Lord appeared. Moses and Aaron went out in front of the Tent of Meeting and the Lord said to Moses, "Get away from this assembly so that I can put an end to them at once." And Moses and Aaron fell facedown. Then Moses sent Aaron with the censer and incense to make atonement for the people for wrath had come from the Lord and a plague had already started on the people. Aaron did as Moses asked and the plague stopped but not before 14,700 people had died (in addition to those who were swallowed up with the Levites).

THE PRIESTHOOD OF THE ISRAELITES

The Budding of Aaron's Staff
In order to settle the issue amongst the Israelites as to who was chosen by God, the Lord told Moses to get twelve staffs from them, one from the leader of each ancestral tribe and the name of each man was to be written on the staff. On the staff of Levi, Aaron's name should be written. Moses was to place the staffs in the Tent of Meeting. God instructed him that the staff belonging to the man that was chosen by God would sprout. God said, "And I will rid myself of this constant grumbling against you by the Israelites."

Moses did as God had instructed him to do and placed the staffs before the Lord in the Tent of the Testimony. The next day, Moses entered the Tent of the Testimony and saw that Aaron's staff, which represented the house of Levi, had not only sprouted but had budded, blossomed and produced almonds. Then Moses brought out all the staffs from the Lord's presence to all the Israelites and they saw what had happened. The Lord said to Moses, "Put back Aaron's staff in front of the Testimony, to be kept as a sign to the rebellious. This will put an end to their grumbling against me, so that they will not die." But the Israelites said to Moses, "We will die! We are lost, we are lost! Anyone who even comes near the tabernacle of the Lord will die. Are we all going to die?"

Duties of Priests and Levites
The Lord commanded Aaron that he, his sons and his father's family were to bear the responsibility for offences against the priesthood. They were to take care of the sanctuary and the altar so that wrath would not fall on the Israelites again. "I myself have selected your fellow Levites from amongst the Israelites as a gift to you,

159

dedicated to the Lord to do the work at the Tent of Meeting", said the Lord. The Lord said, "But only you and your sons may serve as priests in connection with everything at the altar and inside the curtain. I am giving you the service of priesthood as a gift."

THE ISRAELITES JOURNEY FROM THE ZIN DESERT TO MOAB

Water from Another Rock

The whole Israelite community arrived at the Desert of Zin in the first month. Miriam, Moses' sister died and was buried there. No water could be found in the desert and the Israelites began to complain and gathered in opposition against Moses and Aaron. They quarreled with Moses and said, "If only we had died when our brothers fell dead before the Lord! Why did you bring the Lord's community into this desert, that we and our livestock should die here? Why did you bring us up out of Egypt to this terrible place? It has no grain or figs, grapevines or pomegranates. And there is no water to drink!"

Moses and Aaron went from the assembly to the Tent of Meeting and fell facedown and the glory of the Lord appeared to them. The Lord said to Moses, "Take the staff, and you and your brother Aaron gather the assembly together. Speak to that rock before their eyes and it will pour out its water. You will bring water out of the rock for the community so they and their livestock can drink."

So Moses took the staff and he and Aaron gathered the assembly together in front of the rock as the Lord had commanded him. And Moses said to them, "Listen you rebels, must we bring you water out of this rock?" Then Moses raised his arm and struck the rock twice with his staff. He did not speak to the rock as God had instructed. Water gushed out, and the community and their livestock drank. These were the waters of Meribah, where the Israelites quarreled with the Lord and He showed Himself holy amongst them. Because Moses had disobeyed God's order as to how to command the rock to produce water, the Lord said to Moses and Aaron, "Because you did not trust

161

in me enough to honour me as holy in the sight of the Israelites, you will not bring this community into the land I will give them."

Edom Denies Israel Passage

Moses wished for the Israelites to pass through the territory of Edom, so he wrote a letter to the King of Edom, explaining the Israelites' struggle in Egypt and how the Lord had helped them out of Egypt. He told the King of Edom that if he allowed them to pass through Edom he would not go through any field or vineyard or drink water from any well. They would travel along the king's highway and not turn left or right until they had passed through Edom. But the king of Edom would not let them pass. He told them that they may not pass and if they tried, they would be attacked with the sword.

The Israelites asked for permission from the King of Edom again, this time indicating that they would go along the main road and that if they or their livestock drank any of Edom's water, they would pay for it. They indicated that they only wanted to pass through on foot—nothing else. But Edom told them that they were not permitted to pass through. And Edom came out against them with a large and powerful army. Since Edom refused to let them go through their territory, Israel turned away from them.

Aaron Dies

The entire Israelite community had set out from the desert and came to Mount Hor. Upon their arrival at Mount Hor, God told Moses and Aaron that Aaron would die there. They were told again that Aaron would not enter the land that God had promised because he and Moses rebelled against His command at the waters of Meribah when Moses struck the rock instead of speaking to it. The Lord instructed Moses to get Aaron and his son, Eleazar and take them up into the mountains. Once they were there, Moses was to remove Aaron's garments and put them on his son, Eleazar, as Aaron would be gathered to his people; he would die there. Moses did as the Lord commanded and Aaron died on the mountain top. Then Moses and Eleazar came down from the mountain. When the whole community learnt that Aaron had died, the entire house of Israel mourned him for thirty days.

Arad Destroyed
When the Canaanite king of Arad, who lived in the Negev, heard that the Israelites were along the roads in his territory, he attacked them and captured some of them. Then the Israelites made a vow to the Lord that if He delivered their opponents into their hands, that the Israelites would totally destroy their cities. So the Lord listened to the Israelites plea and gave the Canaanites over to them. The Israelites totally destroyed them and their towns, and as a result, the place was named Hormah.

The Bronze Snake
As they were travelling from Mount Hor along the route of the Red Sea to go to Edom, the Israelites grew impatient on the way and they spoke against God and against Moses. They said, "Why have you brought us up out of Egypt to die in the desert? There is no bread! There is no water! And we detest this miserable food!" Then the Lord sent venomous snakes amongst them. The snakes bit the people and many of them died. The people came to Moses and said, "We sinned when we spoke against the Lord and against you. Pray that the Lord will take the snakes away from us." So Moses prayed for the people. The Lord said to Moses, "Make a snake and put it up on a pole, anyone who is bitten can look at it and live." So Moses made a bronze snake and put it up on a pole. Then when anyone

was bitten by a snake and looked at the bronze snake, that person lived.

Defeat of King Sihon and King Og

Israel sent messengers to Sihon, the king of the Amorites asking for permission to pass through his country. They told him that they would not turn aside into any field or vineyard, or drink water from any well and that they would travel along the king's highway until they had passed through his territory. However, the king of the Amorites denied them passage and he mustered his entire army out into the desert against Israel. Israel however, put him to the sword and took over all the land that the Amorites had occupied and settled there.

When they turned to go along the road into the territory of Bashan, Og, the king of Bashan and his whole army marched out to meet them in battle. But the Lord said to Moses, "Do not be afraid of him, for I have handed him over to you, with his whole army and his land. Do to him what you did to Sihon, King of the Amorites who reigned in Heshbon." So the Israelites struck down Og together with his sons and his whole army, leaving them no survivors. And then they took possession of the land.

Defeat of the Moabites

Balak was king of Moab at the time of the Israelites' defeat of the neighboring territories and he was filled with dread of the Israelites because of their numbers. Balak sent for Balaam, who was a prophet, so that he could put a curse on the Israelites. But Balaam had heard from God who told him that he must not go to Balak and that he must not put a curse on the Israelites for they were a blessed people. But Balak sent more men to Balaam, insisting that he would reward Balaam handsomely. Balaam, knowing how God felt about the Israelites, assured the additional men who were sent to him, that even if Balak gave him the palace filled with gold and silver, he could not do anything against the command of the Lord. However, when Balaam went back to God, God gave him permission to go with the men whom Balak had sent but on the basis that he was to do only what God told him to do. Nevertheless, when Balaam set off with the men God became angry with him.

The Talking Donkey

Balaam rode his donkey to meet Balak and Balaam had two servants with him. En route, the donkey saw the angel of the Lord standing in the road with a drawn sword in his hand and she turned off the road into a field but Balaam beat her to get her back on the road. Then the angel of the Lord stood in a narrow path between two vineyards, with walls on both sides. When the donkey saw the angel of the Lord, she pressed close to the wall, crushing Balaam's foot against it. So Balaam beat her again.

Then the angel of the Lord stood in a narrow place where there was no room to turn, either to the left or the right. When the donkey saw the angel of the Lord, she lay down under Balaam and he was angry and beat her with the staff. Then the Lord opened the donkey's mouth and she said to Balaam, "What have I done to you to make you beat me these three times?" Balaam answered the donkey, "You have made a fool of me! If I had a sword in my hand, I would kill you right now." The donkey said to Balaam, "Am I not your own donkey, which you have always ridden, to this day? Have I been in the habit of doing this to you?" Balaam answered, "No."

Then the Lord opened Balaam's eyes, and he saw the angel of the Lord standing in the road with his sword drawn so he bowed low and fell facedown. The angel of the Lord said to him, "Why have you beaten your donkey these three times? I have come here to oppose you because your path is a reckless one before me. The donkey saw me and turned away from me these three times. If she had not turned away, I would certainly have killed you by now, but I would have spared her." Balaam said to the angel of the Lord, "I have sinned. I did not realise that you were standing in the road to oppose me. Now if you are displeased, I will go back." But the angel told him to go with the men, but that he should speak only when God told him to speak. So Balaam continued on the journey with Balak's men.

The Oracles of Balaam

Balaam gave Balak five different oracles in relation to the Israelites on five separate occasions. Instead of curses as Balak expected, God changed Balaam's utterings so that all of the oracles were blessings on the Israelites and pronunciations that God was with them and that they would conquer their enemies. He signaled that they would destroy surrounding territories including the Moabites, the Amalekites and the Kenites. Balak was very angry with Balaam but Balaam insisted that he could only tell him what the Lord had commanded him to say.

Moab Seduces Israel

Balaam, notwithstanding the instructions of the Lord, eventually provided secret advice to Balak as to how he could still conquer the Israelites, albeit indirectly. So Balak, upon advice received secretly from Balaam, encouraged the Moabite women to seduce the Israelite men and the Israelites began to indulge in sexual immorality with Moabite women, who also invited them to make sacrifices to their god, Baal. And the Lord's anger burned against the Israelites. He sent a plague on the Israelites and killed twenty-four thousand of them. Eleazar also decided to kill an Israelite man who brought a Midianite woman to

166

his family right before the eyes of Moses and the entire assembly of Israel (while they were still weeping over the plague God had sent and the deaths from that plague) at the Tent of Meeting. God was pleased with Eleazar for he was zealous as God is for God's own honour. So God made a covenant of peace with him that he and his descendants would have a covenant of a lasting priesthood, because he was zealous for the honour of his God and made atonement for the Israelites.

The Second Census
After the plague, the Lord commanded Moses to take a census of the Israelite community by families—all those twenty years or more who were able to serve in the army of Israel. Reuben's descendants numbered 43,700. Simeon's descendants numbered 22,200. Gad's descendants numbered 40,500. Judah's descendants numbered 76,500. Issachar's descendants numbered 64,300. Zebulun's descendants numbered 60,500. Joseph's descendants numbered 52,700 by Manasseh and 32,500 by Ephraim. The descendants of Benjamin were 45,600. Dan's descendants numbered 64,400. Asher's descendants numbered 53,400 and Naphtali's descendants numbered 45,400. The total number of the men in Israel was 601, 730. Again, the Levites of the tribe of Levi were not counted in the census.

Division of Land
The Lord commanded Moses to allot the land as an inheritance to the people based on the number of names. The larger groups were to be given a larger inheritance and the smaller groups, a smaller one. The land was to be distributed by lot amongst the larger and smaller groups.

LAWS ON INHERITANCE FOR THE ISRAELITES

The daughters of Zelophehad, a descendant of Manasseh (son of Joseph), belonged to the clan of Manasseh. There were five of them and their names were Mahlah, Noah, Hoglah, Milcah and Tirzah. They all approached the entrance of the Tent of Meeting and stood before Moses, Eleazar, the priest and the leaders of the whole assembly. They told the assembly that their father had died in the desert. They made it clear that he was not amongst those who banded together against the Lord and were swallowed up by the earth. He died for his own sins but he left no sons. They asked the question, "Why should our father's name disappear from his clan because he had no sons? Give us property amongst our father's relatives."

So Moses brought their case before the Lord and the Lord said to him, "What Zelophehad's daughters are saying is right. You must certainly give them property as an inheritance amongst their father's relatives and turn their father's inheritance over to them." Then the Lord said to Moses, "Say to the Israelites: 'If a man dies and leaves no son, turn his inheritance over to his daughter. If he has no daughters, give his inheritance to his brothers. If he has no brothers, give his inheritance to his father's brothers. If his father had no brothers, give the inheritance to the nearest relative in his clan, that he may possess it. This is to be a legal requirement for the Israelites, as the Lord commanded Moses.'"

JOSHUA IS CHOSEN

Moses Instructed to View the Promised Land
The Lord said to Moses, "Go up this mountain in the Abarim range and see the land I have given the Israelites. After you have seen it, you too will be gathered to your people, as your brother Aaron was, for when the community rebelled at the waters in the Desert of Zin, both of you disobeyed my command to honour me as holy before their eyes." Moses said to the Lord, "May the Lord, the God of the spirits of all mankind, appoint a man over this community to go out and come in before them, one who will lead them out and bring them in, so the Lord's people will not be like sheep without a shepherd."

God Chooses Joshua
So the Lord said to Moses, "Take Joshua son of Nun, a man in whom is the Spirit, and lay your hand on him. Have him stand before Eleazar the priest and the entire assembly and commission him in their presence. Give him some of your authority so that the whole Israelite community will obey him. He is to stand before Eleazar the priest, who will obtain decisions for him by inquiring before the Lord. At his command, the entire community of the Israelites will go out, and at his command they will come in." Moses did as the Lord commanded him. He took Joshua and made him stand before Eleazar the priest and the whole assembly. Then Eleazar laid hands on him and commissioned him, as the Lord instructed through Moses.

Vengeance on the Midianites
The Lord said to Moses, "Take vengeance on the Midianites for the Israelites. After that, you will be gathered to your people." The Israelites fought against the Midianites and killed every man including the five kings of Midian. They also killed Balaam. However, they captured

the Midianite women and children and all their herds, flocks and goods. When they returned, Moses was angry and asked them why they allowed the women to live. He reminded them that those were the same women that followed Balaam's advice and were the means of turning the Israelites away from the Lord. They were therefore instructed to kill all the boys and any woman who had slept with a man. The girls who had not been touched could be kept. They were also to purify themselves, all the garments and anything made of leather, metal, wood and goat hair.

STORIES OF DEUTERONOMY

The word "Deuteronomy" is taken from the Greek word for "the second law" or "the law repeated". The book records the forceful presentation of the most important aspects of the laws the Israelites were expected to follow once they arrived in the Promised Land. Moses spoke in the eleventh month of the fortieth year after the Israelites left Egypt. In the book of Deuteronomy, Moses is very earnest to warn the Israelites against the sins which had kept their forefathers from entering the Promised Land. The book also deals with the blessings attached to obedience and the curses associated with disobedience. Moses also encourages the people to follow their new leader, Joshua and to go across and take the land which had been promised to Abraham. The laws were written down and turned over to the priests. The book also highlights God's discussion with Moses in which God indicated that Moses would die before the Israelites reached the Promised Land and that Joshua was to be prepared to lead the people to the Promised Land. In chapter 32, Moses records a song which God instructed him to leave for the people so that they could learn it and which was to serve as a witness for God against them. The final chapter gives a brief account of the death of Moses, the greatest prophet and leader ever to have emerged from Israel. The principles derived from the stories are still applicable today as they teach on the value of blessings for obedience, curses for disobedience, leadership, succession planning and preparing for and facing destiny.

PREPARING FOR THE PROMISED LAND

Reflections

Moses reminded the Israelites of their journey from Egypt. He reminded them that following the journey from Horeb, the Lord kept the current generation from seeing the Promised Land because of their disobedient behaviour and that after thirty-eight years in the wilderness, the Lord was now ready for them to cross the Jordan by way of Moab. He reminded them of how they defeated Sihon, the Amorite king and Og, the king of Bashan. He reminded them of when spies were sent out to spy out the land of Canaan and that God promised them that they would possess the land. He spoke to them about their many rebellions and how it caused them to wander in the desert for long periods of time.

Moses Forbidden to Cross the Jordan

He also told the people that he requested of God that he saw the Promised Land, but that the Lord had forbidden him because the Lord was angry with him as a result of the behavior of the people. Moses tried to change the mind of the Lord about seeing the Promised Land, but the Lord then instructed Moses not to speak to Him any more about it. God told him that he would look at the land with his own eyes, but he would not cross the Jordan and he would not enter the land. Moses was commanded to commission Joshua and encourage and strengthen him, for Joshua would lead the Israelites across and would cause them to inherit the land. Moses therefore told the Israelites that he commanded Joshua not to be afraid of any king who possessed any of the kingdoms of the land where they were going. He had seen what the Lord did with Sihon and Og and He would do the same to all the kingdoms where the Israelites were going.

172

Decrees and Laws

Moses reiterated the commandments of the Lord and asked the Israelites to ensure that they obeyed them. He reminded them of what the Lord did to the people who began to worship Baal but that those who held fast to the Lord, their God, were still alive. He reiterated to the people that observance of the laws which their God had set down would show wisdom and understanding to other nations and those nations would know that Israel is a great nation to have its God near it, once its people prayed to Him. He urged them not to forget the things their eyes had seen and not to let those things slip from their heart. Moreover, they were to teach them to their children and their children after them.

Idolatry Forbidden

Moses also reminded the Israelites about the time when the Lord spoke to the Israelites out of fire. The Lord forbade them from being corrupt and from making for themselves any idol, or any image of any shape, whether formed like a man or a woman or like any animal on earth or any bird that flew in the air, or like any creature that moved along the ground or any fish in the waters below. He told them that when they looked up in the sky and saw the sun, the moon and the stars—all the heavenly array—that they should not be enticed into bowing down to them and worshipping things the Lord their God had apportioned to all the nations under Heaven. For the Lord God was a consuming fire, a jealous God.

He advised them that if when they arrived in the Promised Land, they became corrupt and made any kind of idol, or did evil in the sight of the Lord, provoking Him to anger, that they would perish and would not live in the land long, but instead that they would be scattered and only a few would survive amongst the nations to which the Lord

173

would drive them. He cautioned them that when they fell in distress from all the things that would happen to them because of their disobedience, that they would then return to the Lord. The Israelites were also reminded that the Lord is a merciful God and would not abandon or destroy them. He would not forget the covenant with their forefathers which He also confirmed to them by oath.

The Ten Commandments
Moses repeated the Ten Commandments and told the Israelites to learn them and be sure to follow them. He reminded them of the covenant God made with them directly at Horeb. He reminded them also that the Lord spoke with them face to face out of fire on the mountain in a loud voice and also how He wrote the Commandments on two stone tablets and gave them to him as the leader to give to the people. He reminded the Israelites of when they marveled at hearing the voice of God and when they agreed that Moses should go to hear from God for them in order to tell them what God had said. They had agreed at that time, that whatever God told Moses to tell them to do, they would do. He reminded them that God was pleased with their decision and said, "I have heard what this people said to you. Everything they said was good. Oh, that their hearts would be inclined to fear me and keep my commands always, so that it might go well with them and their children forever!" So Moses told them to be careful to do what God had commanded and that they should not turn aside to the left nor to the right. He urged the Israelites to walk all the way that the Lord their God had commanded them, so that they might live and prosper and that their days may be prolonged in the land that they would possess.

Love the Lord Your God

Moses said to the Israelites, "Hear, O Israel: The Lord our God, the Lord is one. Love the Lord, your God, with all your heart and with all your soul and with all your strength. These commandments that I give you today are to be upon your hearts. Impress them upon your children. Talk about them when you sit at home and when you walk along the road, when you lie down and when you get up. Tie them as symbols on your hands and bind them on your foreheads. Write them on the doorframes of your houses and on your gates." He reminded them that the Lord God would bring them into a land with large flourishing cities which they did not build, houses filled with all kinds of good things which they did not provide, wells they did not dig and vineyards and olive groves they did not plant. They were warned however, to be careful that when they ate and were satisfied, that they did not forget the Lord, who brought them out of Egypt, out of the land of slavery.

Moses warned, "Fear the Lord your God, serve him only and take your oaths in his name. Do not follow other gods, for the Lord is a jealous God and his anger will burn against you and will destroy you from the face of the land. Do what is right and good in the Lord's sight so that it may go well with you and you may go in and take over the good land that the Lord promised on oath to your forefathers, thrusting out all your enemies before you, as the Lord said." Moses continued, "In the future, when your son asks you, 'What is the meaning of the stipulations, decrees and laws the Lord our God has commanded you?' Tell him: 'We were slaves of Pharaoh in Egypt, but the Lord brought us out of Egypt with a mighty hand. Before our eyes the Lord sent miraculous signs and wonders—great and terrible —upon Egypt and Pharaoh and his whole household. But the Lord brought us out from there to bring us in and give us the land that he promised on oath to our forefathers. The

175

Lord commanded us to obey all these decrees and to fear the Lord our God, so that we might always prosper and be kept alive, as is the case today. And if we are careful to obey all this law before the Lord our God, as he has commanded us, that will be our righteousness.'"

Driving out the Nations
Moses told the Israelites that God would drive out seven nations, larger and stronger than they were in order for them to possess the Promised Land, namely the Hittites, Girgashites, Amorites, Canaanites, Perizzites, Hivites and the Jebusites. The Israelites were to destroy them completely and make no treaty with them. They were not to intermarry with them as they would turn the people to worship their gods. Their altars were to be broken down and their idols were to be burned in fire. The Israelites were not to worship the Lord their God in the way those nations worshipped their gods. Importantly, the Israelites were reminded that God did not set His affection on them and choose them because they were more numerous than other peoples. In fact they were the fewest of all peoples. It was because the Lord loved them and kept the oath He swore to their forefathers that He brought them out with a mighty hand and redeemed them from the land of slavery. They should know therefore that the Lord their God is faithful, keeping His covenant of love to a thousand generations of those who love Him and keep His commands. But those who hate Him, He would repay to their face by destruction. He would not be slow to repay to their face those who hate Him.

The Israelites were cautioned that if the covenants were kept, God would keep His covenant of love and bless and increase their numbers. He would bless the fruit of the wombs of the people, the crops of the land, any grain, new wine and oil, calves of the herds and lambs of the flock.

The Lord would bless the Israelites more than any other people and would keep them free from every disease. He reminded them that they were not to be afraid of any of these nations, no matter how strong they looked as the Lord their God was a great and awesome God and would deliver the nations over to them.

Do Not Forget the Lord
Moses said, "Be careful to follow every command I am giving you today, so that you may live and increase and may enter and possess the land that the Lord promised on oath to your forefathers." He reminded them of how God led them in the desert for forty years to humble and test them in order to know what was in their hearts and to know whether they would keep His commands. He reminded them that God caused them to hunger and then fed them with manna from Heaven (which was not known to them before) as He wanted to teach them that man should not live on bread alone but on every word that proceeded from the mouth of the Lord. Yet, he reminded them that their clothes did not wear out and their feet did not swell all those forty years. He said, "We must know that as a man disciplines his son, so the Lord God disciplines us."

Moses warned, "Observe the commands of the Lord our God, walking in his ways and revering him. For the Lord your God is bringing you into a good land—a land with streams and pools of water, with springs flowing in the valleys and hills; a land with wheat and barley, vines and fig trees, pomegranates, olive oil and honey; a land where bread will not be scarce and you will lack nothing; a land where the rocks are iron and you can dig copper out of the hills. When you have eaten and are satisfied, praise the Lord your God for the good land he has given you. Be careful that you do not forget the Lord your God, failing to observe his commands, his laws and decrees that I am giving you this day. Otherwise when you build fine houses and settle down, and when your herds and flocks grow large and your silver and gold increase and all you have is multiplied, then your heart will become proud and you will forget the Lord your God, who brought you out of Egypt, out of the land of slavery. He led you through the vast and dreadful desert, that thirsty and waterless land, with its venomous snakes and scorpions. He brought you water out of hard rock. He gave you manna to eat in the desert, something your fathers had never known, to humble and to test you so that in the end it might go well with you."

Moses further admonished, "You may say to yourself, 'My power and the strength of my hands have produced this wealth for me.'" But he warned them again to remember the Lord their God, for it was He who gave them the ability to produce wealth, in order to confirm His covenant, which He swore to their forefathers. He warned them that if they ever forgot the Lord their God and followed other gods and worshipped and bowed down to other gods, then the Lord would destroy them for not obeying Him.

Not because of Israel's Righteousness
Israel was told that the Lord had given them the Promised Land, not on account of their own righteousness or integrity, but that it was on account of the wickedness of certain nations, that God was going to drive those nations out before the Israelites in order to accomplish what He swore to their forefathers. Moses also reminded them of their rebellion against God when they made the golden calf which caused him to fall prostrate before the Lord for forty days and forty nights, eating no bread and drinking no water so that the Lord did not destroy them. He reminded them of their rebellion against the Lord's command to go up and take the land at Taberah, Massah and at Kibroth Hattaavah and how he had to lay prostrate before the Lord

for forty days and forty nights so that the Lord did not destroy them. Hence, Israel was asked to understand then, that it was not because of their righteousness that the Lord their God was giving them this good land to possess, for their behavior had indicated from all accounts that they were a stiff-necked (stubborn) people.

Fear the Lord
Moses also asked the Israelites to circumcise their hearts and asked for them not to be stiff-necked any longer. He said, "For the Lord your God is God of gods and Lord of lords, the great God, mighty and awesome, who shows no partiality and accepts no bribes. He defends the cause of the fatherless and the widow, and loves the alien, giving him food and clothing. And you are to love those who are aliens, for you yourselves were aliens in Egypt." They were instructed to fear the Lord their God and serve Him, and hold fast to Him. Moses told them that He (the Lord) was their praise. He (the Lord) was their God who performed for them those great and awesome wonders that were seen with their own eyes. They were reminded that when their forefathers went to Egypt, they numbered seventy in all, and now the Lord their God had made them as numerous as the stars in the sky.

Love and Obey the Lord
The Israelites were advised by Moses that if they loved the Lord their God and served Him with all their heart and with all their soul, then the Lord would send rain on their land in its season, both autumn and spring rains, so that they may gather in their grain, new wine and oil. He also advised that God would provide grass in the field for their cattle and they would eat and be satisfied. However, if they were not careful, they would be enticed to turn away and worship other gods and bow down to them. Then the Lord's anger would burn against them and He would shut

the heavens so that it would not rain and the ground would yield no produce so that they would perish from the land that God was giving them.

He told them that the words he was speaking should be fixed in their hearts and minds and should be taught to their children when they were sitting at home and when they walked along the road, when they lay down and when they awoke. In this way, their days and the days of their children would be as many as the days that the heavens were above the earth.

Blessings and Curses
Moses said to them that he was setting before them on that day, a blessing and a curse. The blessing would occur if they obeyed the commands of the Lord. They would be blessed in the city and the country, the fruit of their womb would be blessed and the crops of the land and the livestock, the calves of their herd and the lambs of their flocks. Their basket and kneading trough would also be blessed. They would be blessed when they came in and when they went out. The Israelites were assured that the Lord would grant that the enemies who rose up against them be defeated before them. Moses said, "The enemy will come at you from one direction, but they will flee from you in seven directions. The Lord will send a blessing on your barns and on everything you put your hand to. The Lord will grant you abundant prosperity. The Lord will open the heavens, the storehouse of his bounty, to send rain on your land in season and to bless all the work of your hands. You will lend money to nations but will borrow from none. The Lord will make you the head and not the tail."

On the other hand, he told the Israelites that they would be cursed if they disobeyed the commands of the Lord by following other gods, whom they had not known. They would be cursed in the city and in the country, the fruit of their womb would be cursed as well as the crops of the land and the livestock, the calves of their herd and the lambs of their flocks. Their basket and kneading trough would be cursed and they would be cursed when they came in and cursed when they went out.

Moses warned, "The Lord will send on you, curses, confusion and rebuke in everything that you put your hand to, until you are destroyed and come to sudden ruin. The Lord will plague you with diseases. The Lord will cause you to be defeated before your enemies. You will come at them from one direction and will flee from them in seven directions. You will be unsuccessful in everything that you do; day after day you will be oppressed and robbed, with no one to rescue you. The Lord will afflict you with madness, blindness and confusion of mind. You will sow much seed in the field but you will harvest little because locusts will devour it. You will plant vineyards and cultivate them but you will not drink the wine or gather the grapes, because worms will eat them. You will have olive trees throughout your country but you will not use the oil because the olives will drop off. The aliens that live amongst you will rise above you higher and higher, but you will sink lower and lower. He will lend to you, but you will not lend to him. He will be the head but you will be the tail."

Moses told them that even the most gentle woman and man amongst them would have no compassion even for their own spouse and children and every kind of sickness would come upon them until they were destroyed. He said, "All these curses will come upon you. They will pursue you and overtake you until you are destroyed, because you did not obey the Lord your God and observe the commands and decrees He gave you. They will be a sign and a wonder to you and your descendants forever." Moses was very clear that the Israelites were about to cross the Jordan and enter into the land that God was giving them. He warned them that when they took it over, they should be sure to observe all the decrees and laws that he was taking the time to set before them again on that day.

Clean and Unclean Food
Moses also gave instructions as regards food that was deemed clean and unclean. The animals the Israelites could eat of were, the ox, the sheep, the goat, the deer, the gazelle, the roe deer, the wild goat, the ibex, the antelope and the mountain sheep and any animal that had a split hoof (divided into two) and chewed its cud. If the animal had a split hoof but did not chew its cud, or chewed its cud but did not have a split hoof then it was unclean. **Examples of animals that chew the cud but do not have a split hoof (divided into two) are the camel, the rabbit and the coney. The pig, on the other hand, was also unclean for the Israelites as while it has a split hoof (divided into two), it does not chew its cud.**

Of the animals living in the water, they were to eat of those animals that had fins and scales. Anything that did not have fins and scales was unclean. Birds that were not to be eaten included the black vulture, the red kite, the black kite, any kind of falcon, any kind of raven, the horned owl, the screech owl, the gull, any kind of hawk, the little owl, the great owl, the white owl, the desert owl, the osprey, the cormorant, the stork, any kind of heron, the hoopoe and the bat. Any flying insect that swarmed was unclean and was not to be eaten. However, any winged creature that was clean could be eaten. They were to eat nothing they found dead already and they were not to cook a young goat that was still taking milk from its mother.

Tithes

The Israelites were to set aside a tenth of all that their fields produced each year. At the end of three years, the tithes of the year's produce were to be brought and stored in the towns so that the Levites (who received no allotment nor inheritance of land of their own) and the aliens, the fatherless and the widows who lived in the towns, could come and eat and be satisfied, and so that the Lord their God would bless them in all the work of their hands.

The Year for Cancelling Debts

The Israelites were also commanded to cancel debts every seven years. Every creditor was to cancel any loan he made to a fellow Israelite that remained unpaid after seven years and should not require payment for the loan as the Lord's time for cancelling debt had been proclaimed. The Israelites were told that provided that they followed God's commands, they would be blessed as He had promised, and that they would lend to many nations but would borrow from none and that they would rule over many nations but no nation would rule over them.

They were to be kind to the poor, as there would always be poor amongst them. They were to be open-handed and free to lend the poor what he or she needed. If any ill was shown toward the poor because the year for cancelling debts was near and the poor person appealed to the Lord against the person refusing to lend, the person refusing to lend would be guilty of sin. They were to give generously and without a grudging heart, then because of so doing, the Lord would bless them in all their work and in everything they put their hand to.

Freeing Servants

Servants were to be freed in the seventh year of service and they were not to be sent away empty handed. They were to be supplied liberally from the master's threshing floor and winepress. The master was to give to the servant as the Lord had blessed the master. If the servant wanted to stay, because he loved the master, then he became a servant for life. However, a servant's service for six years was worth more than had been paid to him or her so it should never be thought to be a hard thing to set a servant free.

Feasts

The Israelites were reminded to celebrate the Passover, the Feast of Weeks, the Feast of Tabernacles and the Feast of the Unleavened Bread. Three times a year all the men were to appear before the Lord at these feasts and no man was to appear empty-handed. Each was to bring a gift in proportion to the way God had blessed him or her.

The Passover and the Feast of the Unleavened Bread

The Lord's Passover was to begin at twilight on the fourteenth day of the first month. On the fifteenth day of that month the Lord's Feast of Unleavened Bread was to begin: for seven days no bread made with yeast was to be eaten.

Feast of Weeks

From the day after the Sabbath, the day after the first fruit offering was to be brought, the Israelites were to count off fifty days up to the day after the seventh Sabbath and then present an offering of new grain to the Lord. God also reminded the Israelites that when they reaped the harvest, they were not to reap to the very edges of their fields or gather the gleanings of their harvest. They were to be left for the poor and the aliens.

Feast of Tabernacles

On the fifteenth day of the seventh month, the Lord's Feast of the Tabernacles should occur and it should last for seven days. The first day was a sacred day and no regular work was to be done. For seven days, offerings to the Lord by fire should be presented. On the eighth day, a sacred assembly was to be held and assembly offerings (made by fire) were to be presented to the Lord. The eighth day would be the closing of the assembly so no regular work was to be done.

Judges and Law Courts
The Israelites were to appoint judges and officials for each tribe so that they could fairly judge the people. Justice was not to be perverted and no partiality was to be shown. They were instructed not to accept bribes as a bribe blinded the eyes of the wise and twisted the words of the righteous. They were commanded to follow justice and justice alone, so that they might live and possess the land that God was giving to them. If cases which came before the judges were too difficult, then they were to go to the Levite priests and they were to act according to the verdict that the priests gave and turn neither to the right nor to the left.

The King
Upon their arrival in the Promised Land, the Israelites were to appoint a king of the Lord's choosing to rule over them. The king was to be an Israelite and not a foreigner. The king was not to acquire a great number of horses for himself and he was not to take many wives or his heart would be led astray, neither was the king to accumulate large amounts of silver and gold. The king was to learn the laws and keep them so that he and his descendants would reign a long time over his kingdom in Israel.

Offerings for Priests and Levites
As the Levites had no inheritance or allotment, they were to live on the offerings made to the Lord by fire, as that would be their inheritance. They should have no inheritance

amongst their brothers, as the Lord was their inheritance as He had promised them.

Rules on Going to War

The Israelites were commanded that when they were going to war they should not be afraid for it was the Lord who went with them to fight for them against their enemies. They were told that when they go up to attack a city, they must first make an offer of peace. If the king accepted the offer, then all the people would be subject to forced labour and would work for the Israelites. However, if they did not accept the offer then the Israelites were to engage in battle to siege the city. They were also told that when in battle, they should destroy everything that breathed, lest those that they left alive, taught the Israelites to follow their gods. However, they should not cut down the trees that bore fruit as the fruit of the trees was good to eat, but of the trees that did not bear fruit they could cut them down and use them to build siege works until the city at war with the Israelites fell.

JOSHUA TO SUCCEED MOSES

Joshua and the Israelites Encouraged
Moses told the Israelites that he was 120 years old and that he was no longer able to lead them. He informed them that the Lord said to him that, "You will not cross the Jordan." He assured them that God would cross over ahead of them and He would destroy the nations that possessed the lands He had promised them so that they could take possession of the lands. The Lord would do to them what He did to Sihon and Og, the kings of the Amorites, and would deliver them to the Israelites. They were encouraged to be strong and courageous and not to be afraid and terrified because of the inhabitants of the land, for God would go with them and He would never leave them nor forsake them.

He told the Israelites that Joshua would be the one that would cross over with them. So Moses summoned Joshua and said to him in the presence of all Israel, "Be strong and courageous, for you must go with this people into the land that the Lord swore to their forefathers to give to them, and you must divide it amongst them as their inheritance. The Lord himself will go before you and will be with you; he will never leave you nor forsake you. Do not be afraid; do not be discouraged."

Israel's Rebellion Predicted
The Lord spoke to Moses and told him the exact day of his death and that he should call Joshua and both of them should present themselves at the Tent of Meeting so that the Lord could commission Joshua. Moses did as the Lord instructed, so both Moses and Joshua presented themselves at the Tent of Meeting. Then the Lord appeared at the Tent in a pillar of cloud and the cloud stood over the entrance of the Tent. And the Lord said to Moses: "You are going to rest with your fathers, and these people will soon prostitute

themselves to the foreign gods of the land they are entering. They will forsake me and break the covenant I made with them. On that day I will become angry with them; I will hide my face from them and they will be destroyed." Then he told Moses, "Write down a song and teach it to the Israelites and have them sing it, so that it may be a witness for me against them". The song Moses wrote down is recorded in Deuteronomy chapter 32.

God said, "Many disasters and difficulties will come upon them, and on that day, they will ask, 'Have not these disasters come upon us because our God is not with us?' And I will certainly hide my face on that day because of all their wickedness in turning to other gods." God then gave this command to Joshua, son of Nun: "Be strong and courageous, for you will bring the Israelites into the land I promised them on oath, and I myself will be with you."

Then Moses gathered the elders of the Israelites together and told them of the prediction God had made; that they would become utterly corrupt after his death and turn from the way He commanded them. He told them that the Lord had predicted that in the days to come, they would do evil in the sight of the Lord and provoke Him to anger, as they were a rebellious and stiff-necked people. He also said to them, "If you have been rebellious against the Lord while I am still alive, how much more will you rebel after I die!"

Moses to Die on Mount Nebo
On that same day the Lord told Moses, "Go up into the Abarim Range to Mount Nebo in Moab, across from Jericho, and view Canaan, the land I am giving the Israelites as their own possession. There on the mountain that you have climbed, you will die and be gathered to your people, just as your brother, Aaron died on Mount Hor and was gathered to his people. This is because both of you

broke faith with me in the presence of the Israelites at the waters of Meribah Kadesh in the Desert of Zin and because you did not uphold my holiness amongst the Israelites. Therefore, you will see the land only from a distance; you will not enter the land I am giving to the people of Israel."

Then Moses climbed Mount Nebo from the plains of Moab to the top of Pisgah, across from Jericho. There the Lord showed him the whole land—from Gilead to Dan, all of Naphtali, the territory of Ephraim and Manasseh, all the land of Judah as far as the western sea, the Negev and the whole region from the Valley of Jericho, the City of Palms, as far as Zoar. Then the Lord said to him, "This is the land I promised on oath to Abraham, Isaac and Jacob, when I said, 'I will give it to your descendants.' I have let you see it with your eyes but you will not cross over into it." And Moses, the servant of the Lord, died there in Moab, as the Lord had said and the Lord buried him in Moab but to this day no one knows where his grave is. Moses was 120 years old when he died but yet his eyes were not weak nor his strength gone. The Israelites grieved for Moses in the plains of Moab thirty days, until the time of weeping was over.

Joshua, son of Nun was filled with the spirit of wisdom because Moses had laid his hands on him. So the Israelites listened to him and did what the Lord had commanded Moses. Since then, no prophet has risen in Israel like Moses, whom the Lord knew face to face, who did all those miraculous signs and wonders the Lord sent him to do in Egypt—to Pharaoh and to all his officials and to his whole land. For no one has ever shown the mighty power or performed the awesome deeds that Moses did in the sight of Israel.

ABOUT NEW LIFE BAPTIST CHURCH

Summary

New Life Baptist Church or New Life, formerly the Road Town Baptist Church, has its seat of operations in the British Virgin Islands. The facility which houses the Church is located in Duffs Bottom, Tortola, British Virgin Islands. As God would have it, the site was formerly used by the Government of the Virgin Islands as a garbage dump! The Church eventually acquired the site and broke ground in February 1997. Nine months later, in November of that same year, the Church completed construction of new facilities and relocated to Duffs Bottom. In the process of the relocation and operating under the "from garbage to glory" justification, the Road Town Baptist Church underwent a name change to its current name, the New Life Baptist Church. Bishop John I. Cline is the senior pastor of the New Life Baptist Church. At present, the Church has in excess of five hundred members.

Mission

The New Life Baptist Church exists as the body of Christ to preach the gospel, make disciples, model unity and impact communities for the advancement of the Kingdom of God.

Major Initiatives

New Life Day Care & Learning Centre
In 1999, upon completion of the main church building, a second building was constructed and dedicated, which houses the New Life Day Care & Learning Centre. The day care and learning centre opened its doors in September

191

2000 and subsequently expanded to include a pre-school, a year later in 2001. The day care and learning centre is geared toward children from three months to seven years old. It adopts the British education system and thereby provides tuition and instruction for pre-primary aged students up to Stage II. The population of the day care and learning centre to date is approximately 105 students.

Sister Island Mission: Emmanuel Baptist Church on Virgin Gorda
Bishop Cline's commitment to the "Great Commission" (the instruction of the Resurrected Jesus Christ to spread His teachings to all the nations of the world) fueled his efforts to spearhead a missionary endeavor in Virgin Gorda, one of the sister islands in the British Virgin Islands. With the rallied assistance of other local Baptist churches, New Life assisted in the construction of the Emmanuel Baptist Church in The Valley, Virgin Gorda. The Emmanuel Baptist Church was dedicated on Sunday, June 17th, 2001.

Africa Mission and the Tortola Child Rescue and Learning Centre
In 2003, the Church spread its mission to Africa where it supports a church in Nairobi, Kenya. New Life also pledges its financial support to a school built and administered by the Church and in appreciation of its generosity, the school was named the Tortola Child Rescue and Learning Centre. The school currently has a population approximating three hundred students and moves are now afoot to add another storey to the school, in order to be able to create the spacing required to afford more children the opportunity of an education.

Save the Seed Recreational Centre: Tortola

In 2012, in implementing its Mission to impact the BVI community, the Church completed a recreational facility with the specific intention to reach the youth population in the British Virgin Islands, a generation of British Virgin Islanders which, in the view of New Life, is in need of spiritual attention. The centre is appropriately named, the "Save the Seed Energy Centre". The facilities are approximately thirty thousand square feet and house a gymnasium with modern, state-of-the-art workout equipment, a full-size basketball/volleyball court, a children's playroom and café, a six lane bowling alley, conference facilities, a ball room and a learning centre.

Tele-Evangelism Initiative

In furthering its commitment to the Great Commission, the Church also broadcasts its services not only on the island of Tortola, but also in other islands in the Caribbean including St. Kitts, St. Vincent, Anguilla and Jamaica. Its annual Healing and Deliverance and Power Plus crusades are also streamed internationally and have developed quite a large following of persons, including the New Life diaspora, all of whom are very appreciative of the efforts New Life makes to ensure that even those persons who could not be physically present, could still be spiritually fed.

Partnership with Author

New Life is proud to partner with the author, Ms. Ayana S. Hull and be a part of the publication and distribution of The Pentateuch, as she fulfills the Great Commission in spreading the word of God throughout the world and in a youth-focused manner. We are truly excited about the young lives this project will touch and impact universally.

Church Covenant

Having been led, as we believe, by the Spirit of God to receive the Lord Jesus Christ as our savior; and on the profession of our faith, having been baptized in the name of the Father, and of the Son, and of the Holy Spirit, we do now in the presence of God, angels and this assembly most solemnly and joyfully enter into covenant with one another, as one body in Christ.

We engage, therefore, by the aid of the Holy Spirit, to walk together in Christian love; to strive for the advancement of the New Life Baptist Church in knowledge of holiness; to give it a place in our affections, prayers and services above every organisation of human origin; to sustain its worship, ordinances, discipline and doctrine, to contribute cheerfully and regularly, as God has prospered us, toward its expenses, for the support of a faithful and evangelical ministry among us, the relief of the poor and the spread of the Gospel throughout the world. In case of difference of opinion in the church, we will strive to avoid a contentious spirit, and if we cannot unanimously agree, we will cheerfully recognise the right of the majority to govern.

We also engage to maintain family and secret devotion; to study diligently the word of God; to religiously educate our children; to seek the salvation of our kindred and acquaintance; to walk circumspectly in the world; to be kind and just to those in our employ, and faithful in the service we promise others; endeavoring in the purity of heart and good will towards all men to exemplify and commend our holy faith.

We further engage to watch over, to pray for, to exhort and stir up each other unto every good word and work; to guard each other's reputation, not needlessly exposing the infirmities of others; to participate in each other's joys, and with tender sympathy bear one another's burdens and sorrows; to cultivate Christian courtesy; to be slow to give or take offense, but always ready for reconciliation, being mindful of the rules of the Saviour in the eighteenth chapter of Matthew, to secure it without delay; and through life, amid evil report, and good report, to seek to live to the glory of God, who hath called us out of darkness into his marvelous light.

When we remove from this place, we will engage as soon as possible to unite with some other church where we can carry out the spirit of this covenant and the principles of God's word.

AFTERWORD

The family is viewed in both the Old and New Testaments as a basic unit of the believing community. In the New Testament the image of the family is one of the primary ways in which scripture explains the nature of Christians' relationships with God and one another. A stable relationship within the ranks of family is the foundation of a stable society. It is obvious that this present age is in need of a revival and a return to the basic Bible principles that have served as our foundation growing up as kids.

God has given Ayana a very relevant and real life changing approach to the youth of this day through this wonderful, unique presentation of the Pentateuch by way of clear illustrations and experiences.

The greatest need of our day is the solidification of our families. It's a tremendous catastrophe that faces us all.

We are living in a day of changing values. We've been guilty thus far: of majoring in minors. We are challenged to change and impact a very abusive culture. We are facing a time in which there's a decrease of parental authority and an increase of children rights. It's called the adultification of children.

In this day the whole family's structure has been compromised. We must get back on target as the people of God. This fundamental, fun but serious approach God has given Ayana is refreshing!

The stage of adolescence sometimes called the troubled teen is as normal as the terrible twos of early childhood. While the teenage years are ages (13–19), the years of adolescence vary depending on differing cultures, legal status, and personal maturity.

These turbulent times are highly charged with emotional, social and physical changes that can shatter hopes and dreams of parents for their children—even Godly parents who have provided love and encouragement. Sometimes after going through real life situations with your children you've nurtured, you begin to feel that your teenager may be just the tool God is using to motivate you to place all of your trust in Him!

So we thank God for this chosen vessel that He has called for such a time as this and I congratulate the New Life Baptist Church for partnering with Ayana on this initiative. Ayana's compassion, care and concern for our children and youth of this day is evident! Read, explore and receive this timeless material to help restore the Godly foundation that has disintegrated. There is hope for our offspring, and the hope is revealed in this wonderful book.

—Bishop Darryl S. Brister

ABOUT THE AUTHOR

Ayana S. Hull is a born again believer in the Lord, Jesus Christ and is an active member of the New Life Baptist Church. She employs kingdom principles in her everyday life and is a firm believer that God created His Children to be the head and not the tail. She firmly believes that although she is the product of a teenage pregnancy that caused both her parents to exit their educational path prematurely, she is not in this world by accident. Instead, her purpose was divinely orchestrated and it is her intention to fulfill her purpose by using her natural abilities to the glory of God and to leave her beloved Virgin Islands, and by extension, the world at large, a better place than she found it.

Professionally, she is an attorney-at-law and specializes in the establishment and maintenance of investment funds and other investment products in the British Virgin Islands. In 2012, she authored and published *Financial Services deMystified*, a textbook on the financial services industry in the British Virgin Islands which is utilised by the secondary schools in the British Virgin Islands.

Academically, she obtained a Bachelor of Science Degree in Marketing from Florida State University, a Bachelor of Laws Degree from the University of the West Indies (UWI) and a Master of Laws Degree from the University of Cambridge (Cantab). She is a national scholar of the British Virgin Islands, a UWI Joy & Anthony Bland Law Scholar, a Prince of Wales Cambridge Scholar, a Chevening Scholar, a Pegasus Scholar and is a member of Lincoln's Inn of the Inns of Court School of Law.

Is there a book inside of you? Ever wanted to self publish but didn't know how? Concerned about the financial part of self publishing? Relax. Take a deep breath. We can help!

MAKING YOUR DREAMS WITHIN REACH

JP&C

JASHER PRESS & CO.

Finally! An affordable Self Publishing company for all of your Self Publishing needs. We have the right services, with the right prices with the right quality. So, what are you waiting for?

Unpack those dreams, break out that pen, your dreams of getting published may not be so far off after all!

Jasher Press & Co. is here to provide you with Consulting, Book Formatting, Cover Designs, Editing Services but most importantly inspiration to bring your dreams to past.

And this whole process can be done in less than 90 days! You thought about it, you talked about it but now is the time!

WWW.JASHERPRESS.COM
1-888-220-2068
CUSTOMERSERVICE@JASHERPRESS.COM